Growing up in
THE 1960s

Richard Tames

Batsford Academic and Educational Limited London

© Richard Tames 1983
First published 1983

Typeset by Tek-Art Ltd
and printed in Great Britain by
R. J. Acford
Chichester, Sussex
for the publishers
Batsford Academic and Educational Ltd,
an imprint of B. T. Batsford Ltd,
4 Fitzhardinge Street
London W1H 0AH

Frontispiece: **A "flower child" 1967.**

ISBN 0 7134 1342 5

Acknowledgment

The Author and Publishers would like to thank the
following for their kind permission to reproduce
copyright illustrations: BBC Photographs, figs 40,
41; Central Office of Information, fig 22 (Crown
Copyright); Henry Grant, figs 4, 18, 19, 20, 25,
26, 27, 38, 43, 44, 45, 46, 47, 48, 53, 57; Ray
Green, figs 15, 16, 23, 24, 28, 37, 52; Keystone
Press Agency Ltd, frontispiece and figs 1, 2, 3, 5,
6, 8, 9, 11, 12, 13, 14, 21, 29, 32, 34, 49, 50, 51,
55, 56; NASA, fig 10; National Savings Committee,
fig 33; The Tate Gallery, London, figs 35, 36;
Warner Brothers, fig 42. Figs 17, 31 are property
of the Author. The picture research was by Pat
Hodgson.

Contents

Acknowledgments		2
List of Illustrations		4
1	The Sixties	5
2	In the News	10
3	You've Never Had It So Good	20
4	At Home and Away	27
5	Beatlemania	32
6	The Permissive Society	39
7	The Box and the Screen	48
8	Education	54
9	Sport	59
10	Newcomers	63
Date List		69
Books for Further Reading		70
Index		71

The Illustrations

1	Bob Dylan fans	5
2	Mods and mopeds	6
3	Rockers and motorbikes	7
4	Preparing for decimal coinage	8
5	Playground protest	9
6	Vietnam protest	9
7	A prince for Wales	11
8	Francis Chichester	12
9	Biafra child	12
10	A man on the moon	14
11	The *QEII*	15
12	Aberfan	16
13	President Kennedy	17
14	Churchill's funeral	18
15	A car-worker and his family	20
16	Poverty in Wales	21
17	Holidaymakers	21
18	Political demonstration 1963	22
19	Trainee steel-workers	23
20	Anti-nuclear protest	24
21	A mod wedding	25
22	An ideal kitchen	28
23	Inside a slum home	28
24	Mixed housing, Manchester	29
25	Sunday dinner	30
26	*Ready, Steady, Go*	32
27	Beatle posters	33
28	John and Yoko	35
29	Apple boutique	36
30	Mary Quant designs	37
31	Popular fashion	37
32	Blessing bikes	39
33	National Savings advertisement	40
34	Mods and rockers at Margate	41
35	*Whaam*, by Roy Lichtenstein	42
36	*Swinging London, 1967*	44
37	Popular portraits	45
38	Squatters	46
39	TV and Radio Programmes	49
40	Z Cars	50
41	David Frost	50
42	*My Fair Lady*	53
43	School uniform	54
44	Mechanical calculating machines	55
45	An early computer	55
46	Sussex University library	56
47	Learning about "Space"	56
48	An open-plan classroom	58
49	World Cup winners	59
50	"Stop the Seventy Tour"	61
51	Tony Jacklin	62
52	No immigrants	64
53	A girl at school	64
54	West Indies cricket supporters	65
55	Hospital staff, 1969	66
56	Asians at Heathrow	66
57	Liverpool	67

1 The Sixties

Even before the decade was over people had begun to call it the "Swinging Sixties", though many thought it had swung too far. In a momentous speech the British Prime Minister, Harold Macmillan, had warned in 1960 that African nationalism was a "wind of change" which would sweep through that continent. There were winds of change blowing through Britain as well.

Few doubted that Britain *was* changing, but there was little general agreement about the overall character and direction of the changes that were taking place. The acceptance into the language of words like "unisex", "disco", "denim" and "boutique" proclaimed a change in life-styles which crossed and, in some cases, helped to break down the barriers between classes and generations. Indeed, the arrival of the word "life-style" itself suggested that people were consciously thinking about themselves *as people* in a way which was quite novel. The popularity of "teach-ins" and "demos" and

1   Fans — 100,000 people gathered on the Isle of Wight in August 1969 to hear American "protest" singer Bob Dylan.

the cult of "transcendental meditation" and, at the end of the decade, the emergence of "ecology" and "feminism" seemed to signal the questioning of all accepted values and institutions.

Some acclaimed the Sixties as an "age of affluence". Others pronounced — or denounced — the fact that Britain was becoming a "permissive society". And in 1963 the intellectual journal *Encounter* surveyed the state of the country under the heading "Suicide of a Nation?".

It was certainly a decade of contradictions. The Bishop of Woolwich wrote a best-selling paperback which bluntly challenged conventional religious thinking and asked Christians to be, in the words of its title, *Honest to God*. Many young people responded to this challenge by turning East for their inspiration and taking the trail to the Himalayas in search of enlightenment. Others compromised and stayed at home to become week-end "hippies", wearing beads, sandals and a caftan and eating macrobiotic food as symbols registering their wish to "drop out" of suburban society. Reading the

works of the philosopher Herbert Marcuse or the war memoirs of the Cuban revolutionary Che Guevara, or (and this demanded rather less effort) listening to the protest songs of "folk-singer" Bob Dylan were other ways of showing that one had seen through "the system" and wished only to display "solidarity" with the oppressed peoples of the Third World.

Violence and idealism provided further contradictions among the young. Sea-side confrontations between gangs of "Mods" and "Rockers" became a regular Bank Holiday fixture. The press referred to the members of such gangs as "youths", a word which thus acquired clear overtones of disapproval (e.g. three youths are helping the police with their enquiries about an incident late last night. . .). "Young people", by contrast, was the term reserved for the sort of teenagers who went in for the recently-established Duke of Edinburgh's

2 and 3   Hastily through Hastings, 1964. Police ➤ keep mods and rockers moving — and apart.
▼

Award Scheme and undertook VSO (Voluntary Service Overseas) as unpaid teachers in developing countries.

"Technology" was everywhere acknowledged to be the shaping force in our lives and the decade did witness the first heart-transplant and the first moon-landing. More important for society at large, perhaps, were the rapid adoption of the birth-control "pill" and the increasing use of computers by government and industry. But the effects of these innovations were less visible than the deepening impact of the innovations of previous decades, as the majority of British households at last acquired a car, a refrigerator and a telephone.

There were also many changes in the little things that touch our daily lives. The 1960s brought us plastic milk-bottles and the 50p piece (full decimalization came in 1971), BBC2 and the *Sun* newspaper, *Private Eye* magazine and James Bond films, mini-cabs and the first weather reports in centigrade, Sunday colour supplements and off-shore "pirate" radio stations playing pop music 24 hours a day. Other newcomers were the "two-tier" postal service, electronic watches and the Victoria line of the London Underground.

Politically, it was a decade of questioning and protest, though different people found very different things to protest about. In 1962 girls at Carlisle County High School staged a ten-minute "strike" on the school playing-fields, to advertise their objection to a regulation requiring them to wear their uniform berets in a uniform way — pulled down onto the forehead, parallel to the eyes, with the badge in the middle. In 1965 fourteen men on the Isle of Skye, led by the Rev. Angus Smith, were arrested for obstructing tourists who, in their view, had profaned the Sabbath by taking advantage of the first Sunday ferry service to the island. The protests of the 1960s usually call to mind such causes as nuclear disarmament and the Vietnam war, but in their way these almost private gestures of schoolgirls and churchgoers were also significant, just

4   Preparing for decimal coinage — most people had to learn by experience.

5   April 1968.

6   November 1969.

because they were about immediate and local issues rather than remote or global ones. "Protest" had become part of everyman's political tool-kit.

Internationally, Britain began to adjust to a world dominated by super-powers, of which it was no longer one. That much was clear. What was not clear was what Britain should do about it. Britain gave up most of its empire overseas, and the effort to main- tain armed forces "East of Suez" was abandoned. British governments decided that it was time for the country to join the Common Market. The French government decided that it wasn't. The British people were not very sure about it anyway. As the decade closed, what the American statesman Dean Acheson had said back in 1962 was still largely true: "Britain has lost an empire and not yet found a role".

9

2 In the News

Celebrities

Celebrities are people who are in the news, whether they like it or not. A few, like the Royal Family, are what might be called professional celebrities. It is their business to be in the news. And for the Royal Family the 1960s was a successful decade, professionally speaking. It began with the birth of Prince Andrew (followed by Prince Edward in 1964) and the marriage of Princess Margaret to the fashionable photographer, Anthony Armstrong-Jones (who took the title Earl of Snowdon in 1961). It closed with the heir to the throne celebrating his investiture as Prince of Wales with much ceremony at Caernarvon Castle, and his twenty-first birthday with much hilarity at Buckingham Palace.

Some celebrities achieve fame, only to lose it even more swiftly than they gained it. One such was John Bloom, an overnight millionaire who made his fortune from the boom in washing-machine sales, lived lavishly, and saw his business empire crash in ruins in July 1964 when he was still only 33. In 1969 he was to be successfully prosecuted and fined £30,000 for falsifying accounts.

More enduring fame, however, attaches to the name of Rudolf Nureyev, who made the most dramatic entrance of his distinguished career when he defected from his Soviet homeland in June 1961 while on a visit to Paris. To the delight of English ballet fans, he decided to settle in Britain and made his London debut in November 1961, to storms of applause. A year later he began his famous dancing partnership with Dame Margot Fonteyn.

Hero of the decade for many Britons was Francis Chichester who, at an age when most people are drawing their pension and content to limit their exercise to a little gentle gardening, became the first man to sail single-handed round the world. After an epic voyage of 28,000 miles he was knighted in July 1967 at Greenwich, where the first Queen Elizabeth had knighted the first Sir Francis to sail round the world. And at Greenwich his craft, *Gypsy Moth IV*, can still be seen.

Villain of the decade was Adolf Eichmann, a former Nazi, who was arrested by Israeli agents in South America in May 1960, charged with dreadful war-crimes and tried and hanged in Jerusalem two years later.

Wedding of the decade, in terms at least of news value, if not of splendour, was the marriage in October 1968 of Mrs Jacqueline Kennedy, widow of the murdered American president, to Aristotle Onassis, the Greek shipping millionaire.

World News

News from "Third World" countries — a phrase that first began to be generally used around this time — was dominated by stories of conflict and bloodshed, while achievements of sheer survival were largely ignored. The scale of the social and economic challenges faced by Third World leaders was barely comprehended. From Africa came news of the overthrow of Ghana's "Redeemer", Kwame Nkrumah, and of horrendous civil wars in the former Belgian

7   A prince for Wales — at his investiture Prince Charles made a point of addressing the crowds in Welsh, a recognition of the resurgence of Welsh nationalist feeling.

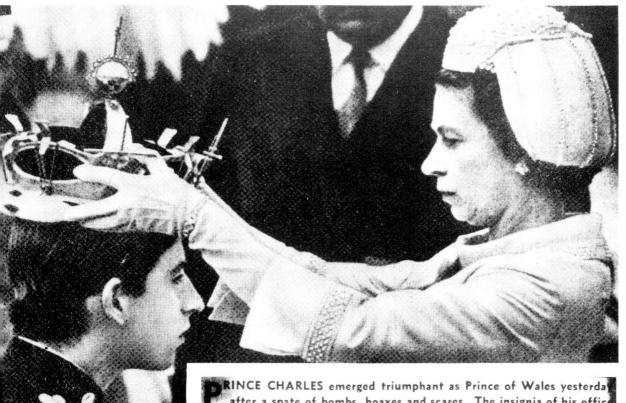

PRINCE CHARLES emerged triumphant as Prince of Wales yesterday after a spate of bombs, hoaxes and scares. The insignia of his office were given to him by the Queen in Caernarvon Castle but he won for himself the loyalty and affection of the thousands of Welsh people who packed the Castle Square and narrow streets on the processional route.

After speaking in impeccable Welsh he switched to English to tell the people from the Investiture dais: "I am determined to serve and to try as best I can to live up to the demands whatever they might be in the rather uncertain future."

This simple statement delivered with youthful sincerity and with an appeal for Welsh co-operation and understanding was relayed by amplifiers to the patient crowds outside the Castle and was the ultimate seal of success on this controversial ceremony.

He touched the Welsh sense of humour when he spoke of the heritage of Wales which dated back to the mists of British history and produced such brave men as " Princes, poets, bards, scholars, and more recently great singers, a very notable goon [Harry Secombe] and several film stars."

11

Congo and in newly-independent Nigeria, where the eastern region tried and failed to become a separate nation — Biafra. India's "Green Revolution" in agriculture naturally received less coverage than its forcible annexation of Portuguese Goa and its border wars with China and Pakistan. In the Middle East, Iraq and Syria endured vengeful coups d'état, while Israel in the "Six Day War" of June 1967 humbled Egypt and its allies by a series of devastating air-strikes.

Britons, receiving so much news from the United States, were also kept fully briefed on the terrible carnage which ravaged Vietnam. Almost none, however, were aware of the terrible anti-Communist massacres which took place in Indonesia in 1965. Perhaps half a million people died, perhaps more.

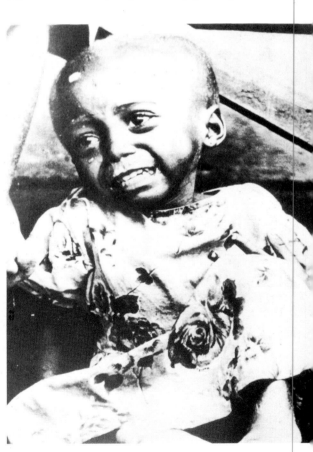

8   Francis Chichester and *Gypsy Moth IV*.

9   The face of war — the disruption of the ➤ Nigerian economy by the civil war brought the horrors of famine to displaced civilians.

China, true to its tradition, kept aloof while undergoing an extended phase of turmoil, curiously termed the "Cultural Revolution". The burning of the British Embassy in Peking by over-enthusiastic demonstrators did, however, do something to bring these events to the attention of the British public.

Europe may have seemed stable by contrast, but the difference was relative rather than absolute. The building of the "Wall" — really a whole complex of barriers and fortifications — between East and West Berlin in 1961, by the East Germans, made clear the continuance of tension between the NATO countries and the nations of the Warsaw Pact. The seizure of power by a group of colonels in Greece in 1967 showed that democracy was not secure even in its birth-place. The growth of urban terrorism in West Germany showed that wealth did not automatically produce the contentment which might abolish political extremism. The intervention of Russian troops in Czechoslovakia in 1968, to help Communist hard-liners crush the short-lived liberal Dubček regime, showed that "bourgeois freedom" still made Moscow very nervous. And the "events of May" of the same year showed that the workers and students of France could still make the bourgeois of France very nervous as well.

If there was a time for everyone in the world to be nervous, it was October 1962. The US government discovered, by the use of high-flying spy planes, that the Soviet government was installing nuclear missiles on the territory of its ally, Cuba, only a hundred miles from the American mainland. President John Kennedy announced a naval blockade on Cuba, to prevent the Russians shipping in any more missiles. The Soviet leader Khrushchev was finally convinced that this was no bluff and ordered the ships to turn back, protesting that the weapons which had been supplied were for defensive purposes only, and agreeing to dismantle what had already been built. It was the nearest the world had come to a direct con-frontation between the two superpowers and it was agreed that the risk of nuclear war had been a very real one. If the Cuban missile crisis had a constructive outcome, it was the decision soon afterwards to set up a "hot-line" so that the Soviet and American leaders could communicate directly in an emergency.

Scientific Achievements

Not surprisingly, the "space race" provided some of the most spectacular scientific achievements of the 1960s. In 1961 Major Yuri Gagarin of the USSR became the first man to travel in space. In 1969 Neil Armstrong, the US astronaut, took a "giant step for mankind", in his own carefully-prepared words, by becoming the first man to walk on the moon. A little nearer earth, the first accurate weather satellite came into operation in 1960, and in 1962 satellite Telstar transmitted live TV pictures across the Atlantic for the first time. From 1965 onwards, intercontinental telephone calls could be relayed via the "Early Bird" satellite.

British achievements in science and technology were less dramatic but still noteworthy. In 1960 *HMS Dreadnought* was launched as the Navy's first nuclear-powered submarine, and in 1961 the world's first hovercraft service began, between Wallasey and Rhyl. The hovercraft, a British invention, was soon to prove its worth, not only as a novel form of passenger transport, but also as an invaluable work-horse in such difficult tasks as laying pipe-lines in Alaska. In 1963 the nation's first nuclear power stations came into operation, making Britain the first country to move beyond the experimental phase in the peaceful use of atomic energy by supplying electricity to the public from this source. In the same year, two engineers at the Royal Aircraft Establishment, Farnborough, developed carbon fibres, which were to revolutionize the construction of aero-engines over the next decade.

Communications improved, thanks to such striking engineering projects as the

10 "We came in peace for all mankind" read the plaque which the Apollo 11 crew left on the moon. (News cutting from the *Evening News,* 21 July 1969.) ▶

TV's most fabulous outside broadcast

By ALDO NICOLOTTI

"IT'S one small step for a man but one vast leap for mankind," said Neil Armstrong as he made the first human footprint on the moon and started television's most incredible outside broadcast.

Millions of viewers in 33 countries, including Poland and Czechoslovakia, sat spellbound as a tiny TV camera beamed astonishingly clear live pictures across a quarter of a million miles of space.

The first pictures of the moon walk were disappointingly obscure but the quality improved as the 2 hr. 47 min. 14 sec. walk progressed.

When Neil Armstrong set up the TV camera on its tripod 60ft. from Eagle, we saw the first clear pictures of another world.

MOONDUST

So good were the pictures that even the puffs of moondust thrown up by the astronauts' footsteps could be seen.

Wisely, both BBC-1 and ITV allowed the two astronauts to provide the only commentary.

The two channels adopted a different approach during their mammoth programmes leading up to the moon walk.

The BBC's quartet of Cliff Michelmore, James Burke, Patrick Moore and Michael Charlton, treated the occasion with the solemnity it deserved.

Not for them the showbiz style of David Frost's ITV programme, Man on the Moon.

Frost turned it into a gala occasion, a sort of VE Day and Frost Programme laced with a dash of Sunday Night at the London Palladium.

Tamar bridge (1961), the Dartford tunnel (1963), the Forth Road bridge (1964), the Severn bridge, the Tay Road bridge and the Tyne Tunnel (all 1966). The launching of the luxury liner *Queen Elizabeth II* and the experimental flights of the Anglo-French *Concorde* also showed Britain's desire to uphold its prestige in international communications. Domestically, the scene was a less happy one. Dr Beeching's drastic reorganization of the railway system led to the

14

closure of 3,800 miles of track and some 2,500 stations between 1963 and 1967. And Professor Colin Buchanan's report on *Traffic in Towns* emphasized the destructive impact of road congestion on urban life and called for the radical "re-pedestrianization" of city centres.

The darker side of scientific progress was also revealed by the discovery in 1962 of the disastrous effects of the ante-natal drug thalidomide, which caused the birth of more than 400 seriously handicapped children in Britain alone.

In 1968 the United Nations, taking a belated cue from Rachel Carson's 1963 best-seller, *Silent Spring*, drew attention to what was coming to be perceived as a major global problem and proposed an international conference on environmental pollution. As the decade closed, the word "ecology" began to be heard outside purely scientific circles.

"Bad News"

Bad news is good news, especially when there is a disaster involved. In 1961 a volcanic eruption on Tristan da Cunha, an island in the South Atlantic, forced the inhabitants to

11 Maiden voyage of a Queen — the *QEII* **leaves Southampton, 1969.**

evacuate. (Most were able to return in 1963.) Europe endured the anger of Nature with an earthquake at Skopje, Yugoslavia (1963) and floods in Florence and Venice, Italy (1967). As far as Britain was concerned, the greatest tragedy was the collapse of a slag-heap which engulfed the village school in Aberfan, killing 116 children and 28 adults. A near-disaster was the partial collapse of Ronan Point, a tower-block in London's East End, following a gas explosion. No loss of human life was involved when the oil tanker *Torrey Canyon* ran aground in March 1967, but 25,000 sea-birds were killed and the RAF had to be called in, in the end, to bomb the ship to pieces after it had caused the biggest spillage to date. Few incidents could have demonstrated more forcefully the dangers of pollution.

If disasters were as disastrous as ever, crimes matched them by being more theatrically criminal. In 1961 George Blake was imprisoned for 42 years for spying for the USSR (he escaped in 1966), and in the same year Goya's portrait of the Duke of Wellington was stolen from the National Gallery. In 1962 Admiralty clerk William Vassall was convicted for 18 years, also for spying for the USSR. The crime of the decade, known immediately and thereafter simply as "The Great Train Robbery", took place in 1963. £2,500,000 was stolen from the Scotland-London express. It took the police most of the rest of the decade to hunt down the robbers, who, for their daring, attained the status of folk-heroes. Nevertheless, they were sent down for 30 years, although the most celebrated of them all, Ronnie Biggs, escaped in 1965 to a comfortable exile in Brazil. In the same year, "Kim" Philby, a Foreign Office official and another

12 Aftermath — workmen clearing the debris which engulfed Aberfan's primary school.

13 The lost leader — President John F. Kennedy faces a press conference. (News cutting from the *Sunday Telegraph*, 24 November 1963.)

OUR TRAGEDY TOO

NOT for decades has political assassination struck more closely at British hearts. The killing itself, in its entire unexpectedness, was shocking enough. But what stirred the pity of millions of us were thoughts of Kennedy's youth, of the recent impact he made in Britain and of the special affection he had for London.

Some people scoff at the "special relationship." British links with the United States, they say, are not and should not be fundamentally different from those of other allies like the French and the Germans. But when Americans suffer a tragedy of this degree of horror it is apparent to everyone that the British share the experience in a specially poignant and vivid way. Eisenhower was felt to be *our* President, too, when he came to London four years ago; and the feeling was as deep as the affection and interest that many Americans feel towards our own Royal family —but quite different in quality. Kennedy was working his way towards a similar position in this country, especially among the young. His personality roused impatience and hope of change and fresh aspirations in our own politics. The slogans of the New Frontier have not had time to leave as deep an imprint here as Roosevelt's New Deal; but they influenced people as widely different as Mr. Harold Wilson and Mr. Edward Heath.

It was remarkable, too, how the British felt they could join in the politics of Kennedy's term in a way that was not possible with the President of 30 years ago. We shared in the jokes and gossip about the White House; we took a fascinated interest in Mrs. Kennedy and the children, in the misfortunes and triumphs of the family. We smiled ruefully at the thought of the Kennedys leaving a hungry and poor Ireland a hundred years ago, only to return there last year as the most powerful family in the world. Whatever we thought of his politics and the methods by which he gained power, Kennedy had become a part of our own national history and he was thought of almost as a citizen of the British Commonwealth.

Doubt and apprehension about the consequences will be felt for a long while to come. We have been too close to the colour problem ourselves in Africa and at home not to dread that the killing of Kennedy in the South may be the first act in a tragedy of violence. We have staked too much on the personal contact between Kennedy and Khruschev not to wonder what can take its place. We were counting heavily on Kennedy's influence to promote the kind of expansion in world trade on which our own growth depends. Policies, it is true, are bigger than men; much that the dead President started will go on; but we must expect during the next year to be sharply, even shockingly, reminded of what the assassination means to the British as well as to the American people. We do more than offer sympathy; we share their mourning and their fears.

SIX-DEEP CROWD
IN THE CITY

SUNDAY TELEGRAPH REPORTERS

MEN and women stood with bowed heads, some silently weeping, as the procession moved slowly into Whitehall shortly after Big Ben had struck for the last time in the day. It was appropriate that part of Churchill's last journey should take him along this avenue which embodies so much British history.

Solemn groups crowded at every window. Others, who had taken up positions along the route before 6 a.m., stood motionless in the chill wind.

As the procession passed the Cenotaph, 150 resistance fighters from France, Belgium and the Scandinavian countries dipped their national flags in salute.

Many of them had tears in their eyes and one murmured brokenly: "It was the least we could do to come here and pay our last respects to the man we loved so much."

Mark of respect

The sombre tones of the Dead March preceded the slowly moving gun carriage and the six carriages carrying family mourners.

It was only just possible to recognise the shadowy figures of Lady Churchill and her two daughters in the leading carriage. But nobody out of respect tried to jostle for a better view of them.

Among the tributes on the Cenotaph to Sir Winston were two from Denmark. One wreath in lilies was from the former resistance fighters inscribed: "From the fighting Danes."

Slowly, the procession moved on into Trafalgar Square.

Impassive crowd

The crowd, impassive and full of emotion, stared stolidly ahead Only once did the external mask slip. As the coach carrying Lady Churchill passed under the shadow of Nelson's Column, a faint ripple of sympathy filtered through the four-deep throng

Mr. Randolph Churchill, Sir Winston's son, led the ten family mourners walking behind the gun-carriage. Alongside him was Mr. Winston Churchill, grandson to Sir Winston.

Ahead, Sir Winston's heraldic insignia was carried by four officers and behind there was the flag of the Cinque Ports, of which Sir Winston was Lord Warden.

In the Strand, where windows and vantage points were as packed as the footpaths, a few women wept openly as the gun-carriage passed.

I heard one woman whispering a prayer. In a window, another woman suddenly dropped on her knees. Hundreds came with their own cameras to commemorate the scene.

Shops, cafes and restaurants were all closed and most had a portrait or commemorative window. Outside the church of St. Clement Dane, a banner was draped with the lettering: "S° many owe so much to you."

And so into Fleet Street, within sight of St. Paul's. Again, hundreds of heads bowed to the passing of the man who had such special links with the newspaper industry from his early days as a war correspondent in South Africa.

Pavements were lined four to six deep for the length of the street, from the City of London's gateway at Temple Bar to densely-packed Ludgate Circus. Transistor radios carried by some of the younger onlookers were abruptly switched off when Sir Winston's coffin came into view.

'The Few'

At the head of the procession, which stretched for nearly a mile, walked 13 representatives of Battle of Britain aircrews—" The Few" to whom Sir Winston paid such memorable tribute.

They walked with dignity.

Black-draped drums beat out the slow march at 65 beats a minute, and as the procession continued down Fleet Street a service in his memory was held in the journalists' church of St. Bride's, a few yards away.

Streaming tears

Nearer St. Paul's now, to the gentle slope of the approach road at Ludgate Hill. The dense crowd packing the crush barrier on either side swayed to and fro.

When the gun-carriage passed, people in the throng wept openly and one elderly man, with a row of medal ribbons on his chest, muttered: "God bless you, sir," as tears streamed down his face.

Several women were carried out of the crowd on stretchers and taken away by St. John Ambulance Brigade members.

spy, fled to the USSR, also to a comfortable exile. 1965 saw the arrest of the child-murderers Brady and Hindley, and 1966 that of the notorious Richardson gang, who tried to bring Chicago-style organized crime to London. As if to underline the alarming growth of violent crime, three policemen were shot dead in Shepherds Bush that year. A topical crime was the theft of the World Cup from the Central Hall, Westminster, where it was on display. (It was found a week later.) The long-delayed arrest of the Kray brothers, who were sentenced to life imprisonment for a variety of crimes, from extortion to murder, gave the forces of law and order some satisfaction in 1969.

Sometimes it is only the deaths of great men or women that bring home their significance for the living. The 1960s saw the deaths of Attlee, Bevan and Morrison, who had presided over the great reforming socialist governments of 1945-51. English literature suffered the loss of Aldous Huxley and T. S. Eliot, and of the American giants, Ernest Hemingway and John Steinbeck. Other figures of world renown who died during the decade included the psychologist Carl Jung, the architect Le Corbusier, the medical missionary Albert Schweitzer, the film-maker Walt Disney and the much-beloved Pope, John XXIII. Many millions felt a personal sense of loss at the early deaths of the American singer, Nat King Cole, and of the broadcaster, Richard Dimbleby. Their voices had been known, quite literally, throughout the land.

But the death which overshadowed the decade was that of President John F. Kennedy, assassinated in Dallas, Texas on 22 November 1963. It was an event which numbed the world. Sir Winston Churchill expressed the general sense of outrage when he said: "This monstrous act has taken from us a great statesman and a wise and valiant man. The loss to the United States and to the world is incalculable". John Kennedy's assassination was followed in 1968 by those of his brother, Robert, a champion of liberal causes, and of Martin Luther King, the civil rights campaigner and winner of the Nobel Peace Prize. Other victims of the assassin included Tom Mboya, the Kenyan politician, and Hendrik Verwoerd, the South African leader. Nehru, Adenauer and Ho Chi Minh all died peacefully in old age.

On 24 January 1965 so did Sir Winston Churchill. His elaborate state funeral was attended by General Eisenhower and General de Gaulle and by the Queen herself. It was the first time that the funeral ceremony of a commoner had been marked by the presence of a reigning monarch, and the gesture was an entirely appropriate one. For, as a people, the British knew that, for them, Churchill's passing marked the end of an age. Ray Gosling, the writer, saw the funeral as a commemoration of the "Dunkirk spirit", even by those who had not even been born then: "Most of us, I'm sure, came not just to mourn or say thank you but to live again those few short days in our lives when we had meaning and glory and fulfilment."

◄ 14 Last journey — Churchill's cortege passes down Fleet Street. (News cutting from 31 January 1965.)

3 You've Never Had It So Good

In 1954 the Conservative Chancellor of the Exchequer, R. A. Butler, had suggested that Britain might double its standard of living over the course of the next twenty-five years. To a generation which had just emerged from thirty years of depression, war and rationing, the prospect must have appeared almost fantastic. But the late 1950s seemed to bear out Butler's prophecy, as a great consumer boom brought television sets, washing machines and motor cars to millions of homes for the first time. In 1959 the Prime Minister, Harold Macmillan, could tell people "You've never had it so good", and in the election of the same year campaigned with the slogan "Life's Better Under the Conservatives". The voters agreed, and the Conservatives won their third general election in a row.

Throughout the 1960s a widespread rise in the standard of living in the United Kingdom continued. In 1960 there were 9.3 people for every car; by 1970 the figure had fallen to 4.7. The average number of hours worked each week in industry continued to decline. Families felt able to postpone sending their children out to work and so the percentage of 15-18 year olds in school or college rose from 19.6% to 30.0% by 1968. Over the course of the decade, the number of people taking foreign holidays quadrupled.

The sudden access of unaccustomed wealth brought new problems as well as new opportunities. Why was it, people asked, that with so many people so much better-off, there was more and not less juvenile delinquency,

15 The good life — a car-worker with his family, new home and Triumph "Herald". Note the newly-fashionable small-wheeled bike and the pedal car without bodywork.

20

vandalism and violent crime? Why was it that, although families were smaller, incomes were higher, and homes more comfortable to live in and easier to keep clean, divorce rates were rising rapidly?

Discontent extended to the economy itself. Politicians blamed each other for what were called "stop-go" policies of economic control. These stemmed from the fact that Britain was both a major industrial exporter and one of the world's major financial powers. Successive governments appeared to be unable to balance the nation's exports and imports while holding up employment and the value of the pound and keeping down prices and interest rates. The attempt to perform this complicated balancing act included "credit squeezes", "price freezes" and "pay pauses" and fighting running battles with trade unions and international bankers.

From the vantage-point of the 1970s, when inflation rose to more than 25% a year, or of the 1980s, when unemployment topped the 3,000,000 mark, the 1960s looks less like a crisis decade than a golden age. There was not a single year in which the economy failed to expand and in 1966 unemployment reached its lowest point ever. A mere 7% was regarded as a crushing rate of interest and, although prices rose by 40% between 1958 and 1969, wages kept comfortably ahead of them by almost doubling.

But there were worrying aspects of Britain's economic performance which suggested that the country had problems which were both deep-rooted and peculiarly its own. Between 1960 and 1974 productivity rose by about 30% in the United Kingdom. In West Germany and France it roughly doubled over the same period. And whereas, even in the depressed 1930s, Britain had enjoyed what was unquestionably the highest standard of living in Europe, thirty years later it was becoming quite clear that it was falling farther and farther behind its con-

16 Left out — like every other decade, the 60s re-discovered the survival of poverty in the midst of affluence.

17 "Space invaders" — British holidaymakers colonize the Spanish coastline.

18 Economic grievances also caused protests.

tinental neighbours. And this was happening just as they were becoming more and more important to Britain as trading partners. In 1958 Europe had taken 27% of Britain's exports and the Commonwealth 37%; by 1970 the figures were 41% and 21% respectively.

The search for the causes of the "British disease" brought in experts of every kind, as the blame fell variously on under-investment, poor industrial relations, irre-levant education, out-dated social attitudes, the interference of the state, the level of taxation and the value of the pound. Harold Wilson warned the Labour Party's annual conference in October 1963 that: "At the very time when the MCC has abandoned the distinction between amateur and professional [in cricket] we are content to remain, in science and in industry, a nation of gentlemen in a world of players."

Some remedial steps were taken. In 1964 a Retraining Act was passed, to encourage workers to acquire new skills. In 1965 the Labour government published a "National Plan" outlining its strategy for raising the nation's income by 25% in five years. (An economic crisis led to the abandonment of the plan two years later.) In 1966 a Re-dundancy Payment Act was passed. Part, at least, of its aim was to make people less frightened of losing their jobs to new tech-nologies. But the late 1960s were over-shadowed by short-run difficulties con-nected with the international value of the pound and the need to "get the balance of payments right" before tackling Britain's more fundamental problems. A few com-mentators saw the discovery of oil in the North Sea in 1965 as the most realistic hope of economic salvation.

Other investigators stood ready to remind the public that "affluence" had not abolished poverty in Britain and, indeed, had made it less tolerable and more ugly. In 1969 the organization, PEP (Political and Economic Planning) estimated that 1% of Britain's population still owned 20% of all personal wealth. The semi-official Family Expenditure Survey of 1970 showed that 9.8% of all households had a weekly income of less than £10 a week, when the average wage in industry was £24 a week. And it was estimated that the proportion of the population living in poverty might be anything from 5% to 15% of the total.

Politics in the 1960s

The management of the economy was probably the biggest single political issue of the 1960s, but it was far from being the only one. The play of circumstances and personal ambition certainly demonstrated the truth of Harold Wilson's saying that "in politics a week is a long time".

The decade opened with the Conservative government riding high on a 100-seat majority in the House of Commons. Labour's disarray was evident at its annual conference at Scarborough, when the party leaders failed to persuade the party delegates to vote against unilateral nuclear disarmament, and Hugh Gaitskell pledged that he would "fight, fight and fight again to save the Party we love". Conservative fortunes began to sink steadily, however, as the economy turned for the worse, Britain's negotiations to enter the EEC broke down, and a spy scandal at the Admiralty and a sex scandal involving the Minister of War made the government look both incompetent and disreputable. This was perhaps unfair, given the real achievements of those years. One was the setting up of the National Economic Development Council as a sort of economic parliament to encourage economic progress through better consultation between government, business

19　Trainee steel-workers absorb the new technology -- too late?

and industry. Another was the rapid and largely trouble-free decolonization of Africa. Governments rarely get much credit for things that do not go wrong, however, and Macmillan himself, dubbed "Supermac" in 1958, increasingly became a figure of fun.

Gaitskell's sudden death in 1963 brought Harold Wilson to prominence as leader of the Opposition, as the worst winter since 1741 paralysed the building industry and crippled transport, to bring unemployment figures to just short of a million, the highest figure since 1947. Wilson's promise that a Labour government would transform the economy through the "white heat" of a "technological revolution", rather than by doctrinaire socialism, contrasted strongly with the bumbling graciousness of Lord Home, who succeeded the ailing Macmillan as Prime Minister in October 1963. A year later Labour edged into power after a close-fought election. Eighteen months of bustling activity appeared to fulfil Wilson's promise of dynamic change and he was awarded a 97-seat majority in the snap election of March 1966. After that, his problems multiplied.

On 11 November 1965 Ian Smith, the Prime Minister of Northern Rhodesia (which was still technically a British colony, though it had enjoyed a good deal of practical control over its own affairs for forty years) had announced a "Unilateral Declaration of Independence". Liberal opinion in Britain and the newly-independent states of black Africa feared that this would lead to the creation of an apartheid state on the lines of South Africa. Harold Wilson promised that Smith's "rebellion" would be crushed by economic sanctions in a matter of "weeks rather than months". It was not.

Meanwhile, the British economy lurched into another crisis as a long seamen's strike crippled the country's overseas trade. In 1967 the government lost five by-elections, was forced to devalue the pound by 14%, and failed again to enter the EEC. In 1968 it lost another five by-elections and was forced to introduce an emergency budget. In 1969 Labour's fortunes appeared to revive as the balance of payments moved into surplus; but it failed to carry through its plans to reform industrial relations, electoral boundaries and the House of Lords. In June 1970 the country turned back to the Conservatives, now led by Edward Heath.

Politics in the 1960s was, however, more than the time-honoured battle between parties. For one thing, new parties entered the scene. In 1966 the first Welsh Nationalist MP was elected to Parliament and in 1967 he was joined by the first Scottish Nationalist MP.

The decade was also notable for its protests. The exploding of Britain's first H-bomb in 1957 led to the founding in 1958 of the Campaign for Nuclear Disarmament, which organized an Easter march from the Atomic Weapons Research Establishment at Aldermaston in Berkshire to Trafalgar Square,

20 Earl Russell (centre) leads a sit-down protest against Polaris missiles.

where there were speeches and a mass rally. This became an annual event which, by 1961, attracted 100,000 marchers. In September of that year a mass demonstration was held in Trafalgar Square, in defiance of a police ban. 1,314 people were arrested in the largest mass-arrest in British history. The 89-year old philosopher, Bertrand Russell, spent a week in Brixton prison as a consequence. After 1963 the movement lost momentum, and from 1965 onwards it was protests against the Vietnam war which attracted the crowds. Demonstrations reached a high-point in March 1968, when more than 100 policemen were injured controlling the crowds which thronged around the American embassy in Grosvenor Square.

Protest and violence with more enduring results broke out in Ulster in the autumn of 1968, as marchers demanding full "civil rights" for Roman Catholics clashed with police and later defied a ban on political demonstrations. Disorder continued as fighting broke out between Catholics and Protestants in different parts of the province. In August 1969 the army took over responsibility for security, and attempts to meet local grievances through political reforms got under way.

Women in the 1960s

The most profound changes in a society are perhaps the most difficult to detect in their early stages. During the 1960s social commentators devoted most of their attention to "youth" and the alleged problems of the "generation gap". The "women's question", which was to dominate social debate in the following decade was only slowing coming into focus.

In 1965 Judge Elizabeth Lane became the first woman to be appointed to the High Court. But perhaps equally significant was the appointment in 1969 of Mrs Yvonne Connolly as Britain's first black headmistress.

Mrs Mary Whitehouse, speaking on behalf of her National Viewers' and Listeners' Association, claimed to voice the unspoken outrage of all those who were dismayed and offended by the rising tide of "permissiveness". Barbara Castle was tipped to become Britain's first woman Prime Minister.

More significant still was the impact of technology. The number of women taking oral contraceptives rose from 3,536 in 1962 to over 1,250,000 by 1969. Over the same period more and more women were also turning to their family doctor for prescriptions to help them "cope". By 1965 the nation's annual consumption had reached 9,000,000 tranquillizers and 2,000,000 anti-depressive tablets.

Dissatisfaction with married life showed in rapidly-rising divorce statistics. The annual average number of divorces doubled from 28,999 in 1955-60 to 55,000 in 1968

21 Even if more couples were simply "living together", marriage remained fashionable — in both senses of the word.

and doubled again in 1972. And, increasingly, it was the woman who was taking the initiative in seeking divorce. In part, this reflected the effect of the Legal Aid Act of 1960 which enabled low-income petitioners to claim their legal costs from public funds. And in 1969 a Divorce Law Reform Act drastically simplified procedures and placed the idea of divorce on a new footing, abolishing the traditional idea of marital "crimes" such as cruelty, adultery and desertion, and substituting the central idea of a marital "breakdown" which could not be mended. In 1970 "quickie" divorces by mutual consent became possible.

While these legal changes may have released people from situations which they found intolerable, they also greatly increased the number of young children from "broken homes" and this generated new demands on education and the social services.

But there was no decrease in the popularity of marriage as such. Whereas in 1931 some 57% of all women in the age-range 20-40 were married, in the decade 1961-71 the figure was over 80%. And over the same period the age at first marriage continued to fall. By the 1960s a third of the girls getting married were still in their teens.

Another comparison over the same span of time reveals a rather surprising continuity. In 1919-20 women accounted for just 27% of all students. In 1967-68 the proportion was just the same. As far as involvement in the labour force went, the great shift had taken place between 1914 and the 1950s, with the virtual disappearance of the Victorian army of maids and "skivvies" and the expansion of female employment in factories and offices. This trend continued, as the female labour force rose from 7,780,000 in 1961 to 8,860,000 in 1966. Another change was the widening of the range of occupations open to them, especially in the civil service and universities. Even more significant, perhaps, was the fact that in 1961, for the first time, there were more married than unmarried women in the female labour force. The decade closed with a symbolic recognition of the new status of the working woman — the passing of an Equal Pay Act. But, as usual, the reality limped some way behind the slogan.

4 At Home and Away

One of the commonly expressed fears of the post-war period has been that the British way of life is being reduced to a dreary sameness through the effects of mass-production and the mass-media. But any market researcher could have told a curious enquirer that distinctive regional preferences, not only in food, but also in clothes, leisure spending and even furniture and decoration, survived well into the 1960s. Indeed, one researcher, D. Elliston Allen, wrote a whole book on this theme (*British Tastes*, 1968), to prove just how vigorously regional life-styles persisted. And the importance of "regional accents" was emphasized by the discovery among television advertisers that "voice-overs" in "received pronunciation" were not always the most effective way to put over one's message. If you are selling baked beans, it probably does make more sense to use the voice of an ordinary house-wife than the voice of an actor trying to sound like a Cabinet Minister. The intro-duction of BBC local radio services after 1970 also helped to strengthen the revival of respectability for regional accents.

Another sign of the difference between the regions, or rather between London and "the provinces", was that only in the South-East did "the arts", in the sense of "high culture", really flourish. Everywhere else, symphony orchestras, theatres and galleries needed subsidies to enable them to survive. The obverse of this situation was the con-tinued vigour in the provinces of such traditional institutions as brass bands and choral societies, which needed no subsidies to help them make ends meet. Sociologists pointed out the not very startling but often overlooked fact that there was more working-class culture in the provinces because the provinces were more working-class. The persisting legacy of the industrial revolution revealed itself in — and was reinforced by — the difference between the percentage staying on at school between the ages of 16 and 18 in the North (23.1%) and in the South-East (36.2%).

Employment and Housing

Another persisting legacy of industrialization was the nation's housing problem. Cruel regional disparities remained evident. In 1967 the national figure for "unfit dwellings" in England and Wales was 11.7%. A break-down by regions revealed that the figure for the North was 15.1%, for the South-East 6.4%. London was something of a special case, with land prices in the central areas of the city running at around five times the national average and a boom in office-building being accompanied by a flight to the outer suburbs by residents. By 1964 it was estimated that overcrowding and the threat of eviction had put 200,000 house-holds in the capital in need of new or better housing. 60,000 families were estimated to be living with friends or relatives and 7,000 people were living in local authority welfare accommodation.

Patterns of physical mobility also con-tinued to show pronounced regional differ-ences. The 1966 sample census estimated that almost 10% of the total UK population had

22 and 23   Not everyone had an "Ideal Home", but even slum homes acquired a television.

moved house within the previous twelve months and more than 30% within the previous five years. But more than half of these moves had been within local authority boundaries. Only 5% involved distances of more than a hundred miles. Nevertheless, regional patterns of in-migration and out-migration reflected varying economic fortunes. The South-East, where the civil service and "knowledge industries" were concentrated, had the highest proportion of non-manual workers and the highest average level of wealth, whether measured by wages, tax returns or the evidence of wills. Not surprisingly, few people left the region. Nine out of every ten persons born in the South-East stayed there. If they did move — on retirement or to seek better housing or promotion — it was to neighbouring regions; with the result that the thinly-populated South-West and East Anglia had the largest proportions in Britain of inhabitants not born within the region, more than 30%. In the North, by contrast, 86% of the population had been born within the region. In Scotland the figure was 92%.

The North, Yorkshire and Humberside, the North-West, Wales and Scotland, were, in descending order, areas of net population loss, reflecting the decline of the old "staple" industries, such as steel and textiles. But it was not redundant mill-hands and foundry-workers who fled south. It was the younger and better-educated members of the community, who took with them the energy, ambition and skills, upon which the economic revival of their birth-places depended.

Employment and housing were the key reasons behind individual decisions to move from one region to another. Employment opportunities depended largely on structural changes in the economy. Housing was subject to the additional influence of government policy. To a very great extent, this was a matter of running to stand still. The number of "improvement grants" made under the terms of the 1949 Housing Act rose from 159,869 in the years 1949-58 to 1,148,705 in the years 1959-68. And between 1960 and 1968 574,000 slum homes were demolished, 2,850,000 new homes built and 1,500,000 people re-housed. Yet the deterioration of existing housing and the continuing rise in the level of people's expectations

24 From back-to-back to up-and-up — tower-blocks in Manchester.

25　Roast and 2 veg — still the typical Sunday family meal.

Food

Eating habits and food preferences are, of all national traits, among the most resistant to change. And the British had long been famed in Europe not merely for the awfulness of their food (over-cooked meat and vegetables, drowned in gravy, and indigestible puddings, drowned in custard), but also for their incomprehensible addiction to it. The writer, George Orwell, had observed of the English in 1947 that:

meant that the number of unfit dwellings rose from 622,000 in 1960 to 1,836,000 in 1967. And the classification "unfit" implied a lack of some very basic facilities. As late as 1966 12.5% of all households still had no hot water tap and 14.9% had no fixed bath.

Their diet differs a great deal from that of any European nation, and they are extremely conservative about it. As a rule they will refuse even to sample a foreign dish, they regard such things as garlic and olive oil with disgust, life is unlivable to them unless they have tea and puddings.

Fifteen years later this was still largely true. A detailed market research survey published in 1958 showed how widely shared common food preferences were. At breakfast, no less than 85% of the population drank tea, while only 4% had coffee. For Sunday lunch, no less than 60% of all households had roast meat and two vegetables, and in more than half of those homes the meat was roast beef.

Another survey, conducted for the *Daily Telegraph* in 1962, revealed how little impact the rising incomes of the 1950s had had as yet on food preferences. Respondents from a cross-section of the entire population were asked by the Gallup Poll organization to say what they considered "the perfect meal", regardless of cost. As the table below shows, tastes had hardly shifted at all between 1947, when food rationing was at its strictest, and 1962, when it had been over for almost ten years:

The Perfect Meal
1947
Sherry
Tomato soup
Sole
Roast chicken
Roast potatoes, peas and sprouts
Trifle and cream
Wine, coffee, cheese and biscuits

1962
Sherry
Tomato soup
Sole
Roast chicken
Roast potatoes, peas and sprouts
Fruit salad and cream
Wine, coffee, cheese and biscuits.

But great changes were on their way — partly because of the continuing rise in incomes, but more significantly because of the growth of foreign travel, changes in women's working lives and the introduction of new methods of food production. Another factor was the growth in Britain of the Indian, Chinese and West Indian communities, whose restaurants and food shops made new dishes and ingredients more readily available.

The "perfect meal" of the 1960s shows that at that time chicken was still regarded as a luxury. The introduction of "factory farming" techniques rapidly made it a luxury almost everyone could afford. In 1955 the British consumed 39,063 tons of chicken. By 1967 the figure had risen nine-fold to 359, 375 tons, representing an annual consumption of almost 12 pounds per person.

As more and more married women went out to work, and an increasing number of homes acquired refrigerators (36% by 1964), spending on "convenience foods" (fish fingers, frozen vegetables, instant mashed potato) increased until, by 1966, it accounted for 20% of all food expenditures. In the same year a leading firm of canned food manufacturers ran a promotional campaign under the slogan "Why bother to cook?"

Oddly enough, more and more people *were* bothering to cook, at the same time that more and more were not. The explanation of this paradox lies in the simple fact that the preparation of routine weekday meals became simpler and faster and, at week-ends and on special occasions, more people felt able to spend time and trouble on cooking dishes that demanded skill or special ingredients. Publishers found an eager readership for cookery books and weekly magazines devoted to cooking.

Whether this new knowledge was translated into practice is another matter. A survey of Hendon housewives in 1963 showed that, although more than 90% of them read the recipes in women's magazines, less than 10% had actually tried a new one in the previous fortnight.

Some food habits undoubtedly changed in the course of the decade. Wine consumption increased markedly. The availability of "instant" coffee made it a national beverage to rival tea. Pizza, spaghetti, curries and chicken chow mein ceased to be exotic, now that they could be bought as readily as fish and chips.

Concern also began to focus on the question not merely of what the British were eating but of how much. It was said that half the nation was over-eating and in 1965 MP Mrs Renee Short called for a national campaign against obesity. Two years later "Weight Watchers" clubs arrived from the USA.

5 Beatlemania

In the 1950s a new sort of human being was born — the "teenager". Some people would have seen the teenager not as a native-born Briton but, like the word itself, as an American import. But, although there was an element of imitation, the British teenager was home-grown, a product of the post-war labour shortage, which pushed up wages for school-leavers, and of long-term changes in the nation's health and diet, which made for earlier physical maturity.

By the 1960s the word "teenager" had passed into ordinary English, and teenagers were increasingly recognized as a distinct social group of great economic and even cultural significance. A character in Ronald Blythe's book, *Akenfield*, a study of a Suffolk village written at the end of the 1960s, explained very well the importance of what had happened: he pointed out that when he had been young, before the war, youth was something you wanted to get over with, so that you could be accepted as a grown-up as quickly as possible. But by the 1960s this had all changed. What one American writer called the "youthquake" had begun to touch even remote Suffolk villages. Youth was now a time to be enjoyed and prolonged as long as possible. People in their twenties and even in their thirties began to listen to what was now known as "pop music" and to follow teenage fashions — the two trends which showed most clearly that "youth" had arrived.

The Beatles — British Pop

During the 1950s popular music had been dominated by American styles and stars, as it had been since before the Great War. Bill

26 *Ready, Steady, Go* — a teenage pop music programme on TV.

27 Early Beatles. ➤

◄ 29 "Apple" — the Beatles' unsuccessful venture into the boutique business. Note the "psychedelic" mural.

that fashion should be fun. Foremost among them was Mary Quant who, with fellow art-student Alexander Plunket-Greene, had opened her first shop — Bazaar — in the Kings Road, Chelsea, as long ago as 1955, and in 1958 produced the first skirts to go above the knee. She went on to popularize knickerbockers, gold chains, shoulder-strap bags and high "kinky" leather boots. By 1962 she was in charge of a million-pounds-a-year business, and Mary Quant clothes were on sale in 150 shops throughout Britain and more than double that number in the USA. In 1966 she began to produce a range of cosmetics — and was awarded the OBE. Commenting on her own impact, in a rather mixed metaphor, she explained that:

> I just happened to start when 'something in the air' was coming to the boil. The clothes I made happened to fit in exactly with the teenage trend, with pop records and expresso bars and jazz clubs.

Lee Bender, another designer, argued that the whole way in which people thought about dress was changing fundamentally:

> I consider that in Britain there is a much greater sense of fashion in the low-price range than in any other country. My mother and her generation used to buy something that lasted for five years. But now it dates you just to be seen in last season's dresses. . . . We're not just selling clothes these days, we're selling fashion.

This "throw-away" philosophy may have been yet another expression of the idea of

▲
30 Be bold — Mary Quant designs for autumn 1969.

31 Outrageous designs caught the headlines, but ► popular "high-fashion" tended to be simple, if daringly short by previous standards.

"liberation". More basically, it depended on the arrival of cheap synthetic fibres like Courtelle and Terylene and the end of the "age of austerity", which, through years of depression, war and rationing, had accustomed a whole generation to wearing turned and mended clothes for as long as they would hold together.

Designers promoted their wares through fashion "boutiques" in Chelsea and Kensington, which themselves became fashionable places to be seen. Provincial cities were quick to copy the trend. "Boutique" originally meant a small shop specializing in a particular style of clothes or the products of a particular designer. But "Biba", the most famous of them all, expanded to the size of a department store before its crash.

Along with the boutiques went the models (Jean Shrimpton and Twiggy), the hairdressers (Leonard, Vidal Sassoon), the magazines (*Honey*, *Nova*, *19*), and products which every woman in the 1970s was to take for granted — hair lacquer, moisturizing cream, hair pieces, tights and lip-gloss.

The real tribute to the power of this revolution in British fashion was the fact that Paris, formerly unchallenged, felt that it had to respond. The famed couturier Balenciaga refused to, and closed his business in 1968. But a generation of brilliant young designers did take up the challenge. And Courrèges, Ungaro, Cardin and Saint Laurent were to become the commanding figures of the 1970s and 1980s.

All this was striking enough, but what caused the most comment was the emergence of flamboyant men's fashions, which seemed to echo the dandified days of the Regency. By 1966 Carnaby Street had 17 boutiques and 13 of them catered for men. The tycoon behind them was John Stephen, master-mind of the "Lord John" chain. Suddenly, men were wearing velvet and lace, Chelsea boots with "Cuban" heels, tight, bell-bottom trousers in denim or even suede, Indian "cheese-cloth" shirts, shaggy "Afghan" coats and shoulder-length hair. That these changes amounted to a real revolution can be judged from the fact that, ten years before, any one of them would have seemed extraordinary and, ten years later, they would just have seemed normal — or even rather old-fashioned.

6 The Permissive Society

It has been said that, because the British dislike the very idea of revolutions, they disguise them from themselves by calling them reforms. This may help to explain why the many changes in the law which took place in the 1960s caused such controversy at the time. Their supporters saw them as rightful extensions of liberty, long-overdue reforms; their opponents saw them

32 Blessing bikes. Attempts by traditional institutions like the Church to come to terms with new social problems and attitudes were dismissed by many of their own supporters as mere "trendiness".

as a disastrous "lowering of standards", undermining all decent moral values, a truly destructive revolution against the wisdom of the past. But the trend continued under both Conservative and Labour governments; and the divisions on many issues were seen as matters of conscience which cut right across traditional party lines.

Bingo, Betting and "Ernie"

1960 saw the passing of a Betting and Gaming Act which legalized bingo. This led to a tremendous growth in the popularity of the only pastime to cater directly for the least "emancipated" section of British society —

Tuck a bit away

with a moth-proof-rustproof-huge-prize-giving-completely-fair-burglarproof-electronic-fun-giving-safe-as-houses character called Ernie

*It would be idiotic not to give yourself a chance to win one of the huge cash prizes every month. £25,000 every three months! £1 units. £1,000 maximum holding. Ask about Premium Bonds at your bank or Post Office.

Whatever and however you save – put a bit in PREMIUM SAVINGS BONDS

National Savings Security

middle-aged, working-class women. Many of the cinemas which were being closed, under the impact of television, found a new lease of life as bingo halls.

The Act also legalized betting shops, and by 1965 there were 15,000 of them. This meant that the police were released from the traditional task of harassing "bookie's runners" passing betting-slips in the street. (Before the Act it had been illegal to take money for bets, except at an actual race-course or dog track.)

In 1963 casino gambling was legalized, a boon to Britain's growing international tourist trade. At the same time, the government itself decided to get in on the act and introduced "Premium Bonds", as a rather bogus form of saving. Because they paid no interest, their actual value was eroded each year by continuing inflation. But they did bring with them the thrill of a monthly "flutter", thanks to the services of "Ernie", probably the first computer in Britain to acquire a personality — another sign of the times.

Radical Moves?

A much more serious measure was passed in 1965 — the abolition of the death sentence for an experimental period of five years. In 1967 homosexual acts between consenting male adults ceased to be a criminal offence. Few people may have been affected by this legislation, but many were appalled that such matters should be openly discussed. In 1969 abortion was made legal, providing that certain conditions were fulfilled. As the "women's movement" gathered strength in the 1970s, further changes in the law relating to abortion were to lead to fierce debate between radical feminists and supporters of the "right to life" of the unborn child. In 1969, also, the abolition of the death penalty was made permanent by Parliament,

33 National Savings advertisement 1967.

34 Battle of the Beaches — mods charge fleeing rockers at Margate, 1964.

despite the fact that public opinion in the country at large was strongly in favour of keeping it.

This variance between Parliamentary and public opinion could perhaps also be seen in another measure passed in that year — the lowering of the voting age from 21 to 18. It was the first time in British history that the franchise had been enlarged without direct pressure from the group which benefited. Contrary to many predictions, it did not unleash a tidal wave of radicalism. The new voters tended to vote for the traditional parties, in almost exactly the same proportions as their parents had done.

Crime and Violence

Meanwhile, crime figures continued to rise. In 1964, for the first time, a million indictable offences were recorded. Particular concern was caused by the disproportionate rise in crimes of violence, crimes involving young offenders, the growth of gangs seeking to promote "organized crime" through protection rackets and drug-trafficking, and the increasing willingness of "professional" criminals to carry guns — and to use them. By 1963, the prevention of crime and the treatment of offenders was estimated to be costing taxpayers £100,000,000 a year.

Over the course of the following five years, the number of probation officers almost doubled. In 1964 the government proposed

41

the introduction of a scheme to compensate victims of criminal violence. In 1967 a new Criminal Justice Act abolished corporal punishment in prisons and introduced majority verdicts in jury trials. These and many other changes in the administration of the law were intended to make it less savage but more sure.

And, to deal with the alarming growth in drunken driving, technology was brought to the aid of the patrolman, in the shape of the "breathalyser", also in 1967.

The annual report of the Metropolitan Police Commissioner for that year revealed that, over the course of the previous ten years, London's "crime-rate" had increased by more than 124%

Lady Chatterley

It was sex, however, rather than violence, which provoked the most outspoken reactions; and not sex involving real people, but sex on the stage, on the screen, large or small, or even sex in books. "The arts" constitute something of a minority cult in Britain and do not normally attract the interest of "ordinary people". But when they appear to flout or confront widely-held standards of taste and decency, some sort of outcry is scarcely surprising.

The decade began with a prosecution being brought against Penguin Books, for publishing D. H. Lawrence's tale of illicit passion, *Lady Chatterley's Lover*. The text used numerous "four-letter words" and was explicit in its descriptions of sexual love. In November 1960 the jury decided, in what was seen as an important test-case, that the book was not "obscene" in the sense of having a tendency to "deprave and corrupt". Penguin Books thereupon opened the doors of their warehouses and sold several hundred thousand copies of a work which most people would never otherwise have heard of. Other publishers were eager to take advantage of this new opportunity for profits and scoured the indexes of censored books for

likely titles. *Lady Chatterley* was followed by the *Kama Sutra*, an ancient Hindu manual of sexual techniques, and *The Memoirs of Fanny Hill*, the alleged autobiography of a seventeenth-century prostitute.

The Theatre

In the 1950s the theatre had appeared to be preoccupied with what its critics called "kitchen-sink drama", in which domestic situations were treated in an extreme way, with the emphasis on swearing, squalor, desperation and despair. In the 1960s new dramatic themes caught the attention of those who did not normally go to the theatre themselves, but read about it when their newspapers thought they ought to be shocked. *The Representative* attacked Pope Pius XII for failing to condemn Hitler's atrocities forcefully enough. The Royal Shakespeare Company presented a whole

series of plays which together made up a "season of cruelty", by portraying cruelty in as many different scenes and situations as possible. John Osborne's *A Patriot for Me* and Frank Marcus's *The Killing of Sister George* dealt frankly with male and female homosexuality. And Edward Bond's *Saved* dealth with brutality by showing a baby being stoned to death on the stage. The rock musical *Hair* (1967) combined nudity, four-letter words and the hippy philosophy of universal love to make a lot of money for its backers.

Some people were outraged by these happenings. Others were cheered by the fact that the 1960s also saw the abolition of censorship in the theatre. No longer could the Lord Chamberlain's Office order changes in a play before it was performed; although action might still be taken afterwards, through a private prosecution by a member of the audience.

More important still, the decade saw the establishment at last of the long-awaited National Theatre, under the direction of Sir Laurence Olivier, and the opening of new theatres in Chichester, Croydon, Guildford, Leicester, Nottingham, Birmingham and Billingham. It also saw the emergence of much new theatrical talent on and off the stage — directors Peter Hall and Trevor Nunn, playwrights Tom Stoppard, Alan Ayckbourn, David Storey and Peter Nichols, actors Ian McKellern and Nicol Williamson, and actresses Maggie Smith and Vanessa Redgrave all established or enlarged their reputations.

35 "Whaam" — by Roy Lichtenstein — "pop art" directly inspired by popular comics.

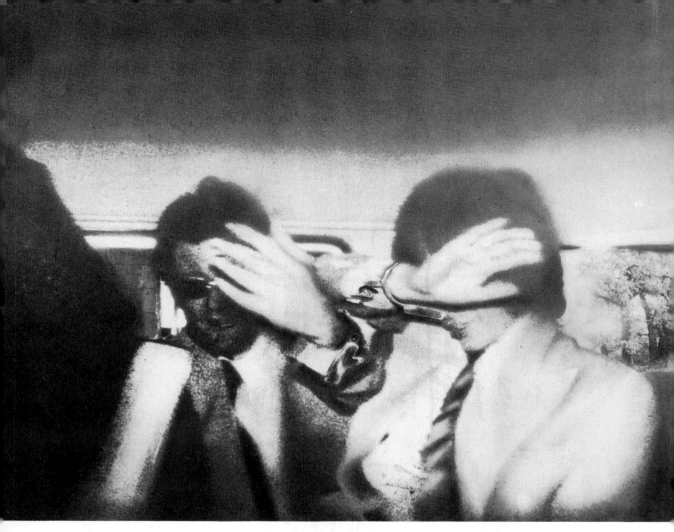

There were also unmistakeable signs of theatrical normality for anyone who cared to read them. The four-hundredth anniversary of Shakespeare's birth saw many memorable productions of his works and *The Mousetrap* ran on and on and on.

"Pop Art" and Poetry

The theatre probably provoked more attention and discussion than the other arts, plastic or performing. But "Pop art" and "Op Art" outraged many, by their claim to be any sort of art at all. And the publication of volumes of poetry by John Lennon, Bob Dylan and Leonard Cohen was likewise dismissed as absurdly pretentious. But the

36 "Swinging London 1967" — a satirical comment on publicity-seeking cult heroes seeking to avoid publicity while handcuffed — presumably on a drugs charge.

real significance of both these developments lies in the fact that they appealed chiefly to the young. And it was the effect on "the young" that "permissiveness" was having that caused the most concern among preachers, TV pundits and the writers of newspaper editorials.

37 Pin-Ups — George Best, footballer (top ➤ centre) and the Queen (middle left) in the style of the celebrated portrait by Annigoni.

Young People and Their Attitudes

Sober sociological investigation was to show that there was not a great deal for the older generation to get worried about. "Mods" and "Rockers" may have battered each other on Bank Holiday beaches, but most young people shared the attitudes of their parents and thought that "young thugs" should be subjected to severe — including physical — punishment. CND marchers and "student militants" soon found that their biggest enemy was not the repression of the authorities, but the political apathy of the masses who refused to be mobilized.

A poll conducted by National Opinion Polls in November 1967 showed that 2/3 of teenage boys and 1/3 of teenage girls agreed that sex before marriage was not wrong. (Another careful study had already shown that the proportion of young people who had actually had sexual intercourse before the age of 20 was almost exactly half the proportion of those who said they were in favour of it — in other words, about one boy in three and one girl in six.)

The same NOP poll showed that 68% of its sample of young people wanted to bring back the death penalty and 30% wanted to "send back" coloured immigrants.

Asked to name their most popular personality, they produced a "Top Ten" which put "Mum" first and "Dad" fifth, with the Queen (number two) and Harold Wilson (number four) inbetween. Other members of the top ten included Bobby Charlton, Prince Philip and President Lyndon Johnson.

Nor were their hopes for the future unrealistic. Professor C. A. Mace noted in 1962 that:

Few young people have the ambition to become millionaires, peers, film-stars, even Lord Mayors of London. They are on the whole realistic, setting their sights to the reasonably attainable.

The sociologist Philip Abrams declared in 1964:

We have produced a satisfied generation. 'Satisfied', 'I'm satisfied', 'This is a good country', 'All things considered I'm quite satisfied', 'Quite satisfied' are the stock responses of the under 25s. Study after study has documented the growth and spread of this mood. Through it, as though round the edge of rose-tinted blinkers, the young peer dimly at contemporary Britain.

But, if there was no cauldron of seething discontent about to boil over into full-scale social revolution, there were still traditional black spots which were just getting blacker. The *Observer* reported of Glasgow in 1965 that:

An average of ten shop windows are being shattered every night in the week. The culprits are invariably teenagers and mostly it is a case of smash without grab. In the first three weeks of March a total of 109 teenagers were arrested, 46 of these were carrying offensive weapons, chiefly flick-knives; some of them were aged between 12 and 14.

And new black spots were being created. The *Times* reported of Kirkby New Town, outside Liverpool, in the same year that:

Shop windows are shattered with monotonous regularity, telephone kiosks are damaged at the rate of one a day and the windows of unoccupied buildings have to be protected by corrugated iron.

Outside "Swinging London" there were still millions of teenagers with "nowhere to go", "waiting for something to happen".

◄ 38 Squatters.

7 The Box and the Screen

In 1950 less than one home in twenty in Britain had television. But by 1953 the coronation of Elizabeth II was watched by 25,000,000 viewers; half of the entire population managed one way or another to put themselves in front of a set. In 1955 the BBC's monopoly was ended by the coming of Independent Television. By 1957 more than half the homes in Britain had acquired a television set, and by 1958 television programmes could be received in virtually every part of the United Kingdom. In 1959 the transmission of TV news films by transatlantic telephone cable was pioneered by the BBC. In 1960 the Corporation moved from Alexandra Palace in North London to its new Television Centre in Shepherd's Bush in West London, and the following year celebrated the twenty-fifth anniversary of what had begun in 1936 as the world's first television service. Technical improvement continued, with the introduction of colour television in 1967. By 1970 half a million colour television sets were in operation.

TV Programmes of the 1960s

If the BBC still made the pace as far as technology went, ITV certainly threw down the gauntlet with new types of programme and presentation. Its cash-prize quiz shows were criticized by the intellectuals, but drew large audiences. Its pioneering efforts in providing live coverage of the annual autumn conferences of the political parties and the Trades Union Congress were recognized, on the other hand, as a major advance.

Television in the 1960s acquired a new realism — whether dealing with crime, politics or human relations. During the 1950s, for instance, the image of the police had been built around the veteran actor Jack Warner's portrayal of PC George Dixon, the fatherly guardian of order in Dock Green, a mythical district of London's East End. In 1962 *Z Cars* began. The old-fashioned "copper on the beat" was replaced by tough, young trouble-shooters in squad cars, operating against the background of "Newtown", an imaginary but realistic northern city. Perhaps this reflected a real change between the two decades, but the contrast seemed striking at the time. The day after the first *Z Cars* programme was broadcast, the Chief Constable of Lancashire drove down to London to protest in person about the way the police were being portrayed. Unfortunately for him, *Z Cars* was a huge success with the viewers and went on for another five hundred episodes, to be followed by *Softly, Softly*, which, if anything, was even more direct in its attempt to give police drama a cutting edge.

Z Cars made some people uncomfortable. But what really upset them was *That Was The Week That Was*, a late-night programme of songs and sketches that only ran for eight months, but built up an audience of 12,000,000 and made "satire" a household word. The main presenters were David Frost and Ned Sherrin. To *TW3* nothing was sacred — politicians, churchmen, trade unionists and broadcasters themselves could all be laughed at. There were many cries

TELEVISION PROGRAMMES

B.B.C. 1

10.30 a.m.-11.30, Morning Service from Liskeard Parish Church. Cornwall. 11.50, Ddoe Heddiw : Welsh topical magazine.
12.15, Ten Composers : Purcell.
12.45, Running A Home.
1.15-1.45, Laws of Disorder : introduction to chemical change and thermodynamics.
1.55, Farming In Westminster: Annual General Meeting of National Farmers Union, followed by Weather for farmers.
2.25, World Bobsleigh Championships.
2.55, " Marry Me Again " (film).
3.55, The World Of Tonight.
4.40, Z Cars (rpt.).
5.30, B.B.C. 2 Showcase : The Massingham Affair.
6, Sooty.
6.10, News and Weather.
6.15, Meeting Point: Failure in Woolwich.
6.45, Sunday Story : " Desert Calling."
6.50, Songs of Praise from Seion Presbyterian Chapel, Llanrwst.
7.25, " Unconquered " (film).
9.50, Dr. Finlay's Casebook.
10.40, News.
10.50, Not So Much A Programme More A Way Of Life.
11.35, Meeting Point (rpt. from 6.15).
12.5, Weather.

B.B.C. 2

2 p.m.-4, Brands Hatch Motor Racing. 7, News Review for the Deaf. 7.25, An Evening with Robert Morley rpt. 8.15, Culloden (documentary reconstruction), rpt. from B.B.C.1.
9.25, Best of Both Worlds—music.
10.5, " The Ambassadors " (Henry James serial dramatisation). 10.50, News ; Late Night Line-up.

I.TV.

London (A.TV.)

9.50 a.m., Sunday Session: Psychology for Everyman.
10.15, Power in Britain : The House of Commons.
10.40, Mesdames, Messieurs . . .
11-12.15, Choral Eucharist from Lancing College Chapel, Sussex.
2.21, Auto-Mechanics: Carburettors and Air Filters (rpt.).
2.40, News.
2.45, Tempo : " The Ring of Laughter."
3.10, The Beverley Hillbillies.
3.45, Police Five.
3.50, " The Spider and the Fly " (film): Eric Portman, Nadia Gray.
5.35, Stingray.
6.5, News.
6.15, Storytime : David Kossoff and Cy Grant.
6.35, Sunday Break.

7.5, Hallelujah.
7.25, News.
7.29, The Secret Life of Walter Mitty : Danny Kaye.
9, Golden Drama: excerpts from famous plays.
10, News.
10.10, Golden Drama (continued).
11.5, Eamonn Andrews Show ; weather.
11.50, Epilogue.

Southern

9.50 a.m.-12.5, London. 2.45, Weather ; Farm in the South. 3.18, Ready, Steady, Go ! 4.14, Bonanza. 5.5, Lucy Show. 5.35-11.48, London (6.5, 7.25, 10, News). 11.50, Weather ; Epilogue.

Home

7.50 a.m., Reading. 7.55, Weather. 8. News. 8.10, Eye-witness. 8.40, Sunday Papers. 8.50, Programme news. 8.55, Weather. 9, News. 9.5, With Heart and Voice. 9.30, The Archers. 10.30, Service from St. Cuthbert's Parish Church, Edinburgh, 11.15, Basil Boothroyd at Bay. ' 11.30, Holiday Hour. 12.10, Critics. 12.55, Weather.
1. News. 1.10, Any Questions? rpt. 2, Gardeners' Question Time. 2.30, " The Crippled Tanker " (Kenneth Langmaid play): Brewster Mason, William Eedle. Eric Woodburn. 4, Home for the Day. 4.40, Can I Help You? 5, Country Questions. 5.30, The Archaeologist. 5.55, Weather.
6, News; Newsreel. 6.45, Reginald Leopold Palm Court Orch., Harry Mossfield. 7.30, Letter from America: Alistair Cooke. 7.45, Act of Worship from Chichester Cathedral. 8.15, Good Cause. 8.20, " The American " (serial). 9, Your 100 Best Tunes.
10, News. 10.10, Instead of Hanging —What? (discussion). 10.50, Epilogue. 10.59, Weather. 11, News. 11.2-11.45, Scarlatti and Granados: Angus Morrison (piano).

Regional Variations

SOUTH AND WEST

10.30 a.m.-11.30, Morning Service: Communion from Bristol. 4-4.40, As Prescribed : request items for patients in hospital.

Light

6.55 a.m., Christian words and music. 7, Weather, News; Morning Melody (7.30, News; Road Round-up). 8.30, News; Record Show (8.55, Metcast. 9.30, News). 10.30, News; Easy Beat. 11.30, R.C. Service. 11.55, Programme news. 12, Two-way Family Favourites.
1.30, Tommy Steele Show. 2, Does the Team Think? 2.30, Clitheroe Kid. 3, Semprini Serenade. 4, Pick of the Pops. 5, Enchanted Evenings—music from stage and screen. 6, Mantovani

Channel Islands

9.50 a.m.-12.15, London. 3, Voyage to the Bottom of the Sea. 3.55, Pop and Leslie. 4.10, No Time for Sergeants. 4.35, Flintstones. 5, Puffin. 5.5, Bonanza. 6.5, News. 6.15-7.24 London. 7.24, Regional News ; " Sea Fury " (film). 9-11.48, London. (10, News). 11.50, Epilogue ; Weather.

Anglia

9.50 a.m.-12.15, London. 2.10, Weather ; Farming Diary. 2.45, " Cynara " (film): Ronald Colman. 4.40, Ready, Steady, Go ! 5.5, Match of the Week. 5.35-11.48, London (6.3, Weather, News ; 7.25, News; 10, News, Weather). 11.48, Weather ; Postscript.

SOUND

Orch. 6.30, What Do You Know? 7, " The Quarry " (serial). 7.30, News. 7.35, Melody Hour. 8.30, Hymn-singing. 9, A Night at the Music-hall. 9.45, When Shadows Fall —music (10.30, News). 10.45, Teen Scene. 11.30, News; Stay Late—music (12.30, News). 1.30, News; Blues in the Night. 2, News, Weather.

Music Programme (Third Network)

8 a.m., News, Weather; What's New (rcds.), 9, News, Weather; The Haydn Symphony—No. 86 in D major. 9.30, Concert Choice, recds. 10.30, Music in Miniature. 11, Music Magazine. 12, " L'Elisir d'Amore " (Donizetti opera). 1.20, Mozart, Strauss, Dvorak; Portia Wind Ensemble, and others. 2.15, Talking about Music: Antony Hopkins. 2.45, Bach: Robert Collet (piano). 3, Schumann, Dvorak, Brahms: Josef Suk (violin), B.B.C. Symphony Orch. conducted by Sir Malcolm Sargent (3.53-4.13, Alec Robertson talks to Josef Suk).

Third

5, Epic Survivals — Traces of the Epic in Africa, rpt. 5.55, " Die Gezeichneten " (Franz Schreker opera): German recdg (6.50-7.5, " The Boat "—Robert Creeley story). 7.55-8.30, The Novelist as Innovator— Laurence Sterne. 9.50, " Merely Players " (Edmund Crispin play). 11-11.15, News.

Luxembourg

6, Beaver Club. 6.15, Spin Beat. 6.30, The Magic of Dean Martin. 7, Jack Jackson New Jukebox Show. 7.30, Sunday's Requests. 8, The Night is Young. 8.45, The Beatles. 9, Kids Like Us. 9.15, Rhythm and Blues Time. 9.30, Ready-Steady-Radio. 10, The Sam Costa Show. 10.30, Sunday Night at the Cavern. 11, Top Twenty. 12, Midnight with Brian Matthew. 12.30-2, Music in the Night.

40   Britain's best-known policemen — the cast of *Z Cars*. Colin Welland (second from left) is now better-known as a playwright.

of protest. One critic described Frost and Sherrin as "pedlars of filth and smut and destroyers of all that Britain holds dear". As a general election approached, the programme was dropped. But television as a whole was never quite the same again. As Charles Curran, Director-General of the BBC, put it: "You cannot expect the BBC to remain stuck at teatime 1935."

Many programmes first broadcast in the 1960s remained firm favourites for years to come. Some seemed to find a magic formula which enabled them to keep going into the 1980s. These included *Coronation Street*, *Dr. Who*, *University Challenge*, *Top of the Pops*, *Playschool* and *Jackanory*. Others which enjoyed great popularity at the time and into the 1970s were *The*

41   Whizz-kid — David Frost, presenter of *That Was The Week That Was*.

Avengers, Dr. Finlay's Casebook, Dad's Army, Steptoe and Son and *Monty Python's Flying Circus*. These programmes were entirely British in origin and, to a very large extent, in their appeal as well. Although some soap operas, like *Peyton Place* and *Dr. Kildare*, were successfully imported from America, and a few shows, like *Candid Camera*, were adaptations of American ideas, the remarkable thing is, considering the vast output of the American television industry, not how many American television series were shown in Britain, but how few. Anyone wanting to argue that in the 1960s British culture was becoming Americanized could find little evidence to support this in the field of television. Indeed, the influence might well be said to have run in the other direction, with the sale to the United States of such ambitious projects as the BBC's productions of Shakespeare or its skilful adaptations of classic English novels, like the immensely popular *Forsyte Saga*, or the *Civilization* series, a history of Western art, presented by Sir Kenneth Clark.

The Effects of Television Watching

By the mid-1960s, "watching television" had become the most important single leisure activity for a quarter of Britain's population, more than twice as high a proportion as for the second most popular pastime — gardening. The TV craze was vilified as little less than a national disaster. In 1962 the writer J. B. Priestley noted accusingly that:

> Most of us are content to stare at programmes we would never leave the house and go fifty yards to see. We watch and listen in an idle dream. . . .We could smile and yawn at scenes of torture and murder. Very little appearing on that tiny screen in the living-room appears quite real. . . . Really good television, I believe, will begin when we have to pay for something, on the night, to see it. We shall give it a

different kind of attention and demand value for money.

Ten years later, Sir Hugh Greene, a former Director-General of the BBC, still found himself strongly in agreement with this view:

> I would think that it would be a good thing on the whole for people if they halved the time they watched television and spent that half reading a book or working in the garden or going for a walk or playing a game. Ideally, yes, they should watch less television.

Television was frequently blamed for the rising rate of violent crime. In Britain, worried researchers carried out surveys to measure the effect of television on the young. They found that they listened to less radio (this was before the widespread availability of cheap transistorized portables) and read fewer comics than their parents had done. But there was little sign that they had ceased to value games or friendship:

> "I don't watch much telly . . .'cause I'm hardly ever in the house . . . unless I'm over at the youth club and sommat's on good, you know, I watch it then, like 'Top of the Pops'. I don't watch much at home though — I'm never in." (Leicestershire girl, 15)

> "I like TV when there's nothing else to do. . . . There are very few programmes that I watch every week." (Oxfordshire boy, 13)

Roger Bannister, chairman of the Sports Council, agreed that television actually encouraged some people to get up out of their armchairs:

> Any governing body will tell you that if their own sport is shown on television, whether it's archery or sailing or bad-

minton or squash, over the next few weeks they're inundated with applications to join clubs and requests for information about the sport.

But perhaps the major importance of television was not the behaviour it produced, but the behaviour it was supposed to prevent. If everyone was watching the box, were families talking to each other any more? And, if they weren't, why should they listen to each other when they needed to?

If the experts disagreed about the effects of television on the public, there was little room for disagreement about its impact on other forms of entertainment. In 1950 almost 12,000,000 British homes held a radio licence. By 1966 less than 3,000,000 did so. In 1971 the radio licence was abolished. The number of cinemas was halved in the course of twenty years, as cinema attendances fell drastically, from 1,300,000,000 a year in 1954 to 300,000,000 in 1966.

The Cinema

The cinema fought back. One tactic was to exploit the trend towards "realism", by translating onto film the sort of books and plays that were still too "frank" for television in their portrayal of sex and social criticism. Tony Richardson's film of John Osborne's play *Look Back in Anger* led the way in 1956, to be followed by Jack Clayton's version of John Braine's *Room at the Top* and film versions of two of Alan Sillitoe's novels of working-class refusal to "conform" — *The Loneliness of the Long Distance Runner* and *Saturday Night and Sunday Morning*. A second tactic was to offer what the small screen by definition could not — sheer scale. American-made "epics" ranged from historical dramas such as *Ben Hur*, *Spartacus*, *El Cid*, *Cleopatra*, *Dr. Zhivago* and *Zulu*, to war films like *The Guns of Navarone*, *The Great Escape* and *The Dirty Dozen*, to lavishly-costumed musicals like *My Fair Lady*, *Mary Poppins* and *The Sound of Music*. British film-makers did the best they could with the money they could raise and came up with *Lawrence of Arabia*, *Charge of the Light Brigade*, *2001: A Space Odyssey* and *Oh! What a lovely War*. Fortunately, they were also able to call on talents like Albert Finney, Sir Alec Guinness, Peter Sellers, Sean Connery, Tom Courtenay and Michael Caine. Fortunately also, the people who did still go to the cinema seemed to have an endless appetite for Hammer horror films, "Carry On" comedies and James Bond fantasies.

42 *My Fair Lady* — a musical smash-hit based ➤
on George Bernard Shaw's play *Pygmalion*.

MY FAIR LADY

From Warner Bros.   Released through Warner-Pathe
TECHNICOLOR (R) **SUPER PANAVISION** (R)

8 Education

The 1944 Education Act promised secondary education for all. But by the 1960s many people were asking whether the sort of secondary education that was being given was good enough. And other people were suggesting that what Britain really needed was better primary education or more further and higher education. Social justice, the welfare of the individual child and the progress of the economy were all called upon to justify changes in educational practice and provision. Enquiries, reports, conferences and Acts of Parliament kept the educational world in ferment. And in the schools some changes did actually happen.

The Comprehensive System

The issue that caused the most controversy was probably the move to "comprehensive education". The 1944 Act had assumed that children could be assigned to different types of secondary schools, quite objectively, according to their aptitudes and abilities — the most "academic" would go to grammar schools, the more practically-minded to technical schools and the rest to "secondary moderns". What seemed to happen in practice was that the established grammar schools survived with very little change, "creaming off" the most able children, while the rest

43   Tradition lingers on — uniforms at Hampstead Comprehensive.

were shunted into "sec-mods". Technical high schools simply failed to develop in sufficient numbers. Selection for the different types of school took place at around the age of 11; and the competitive "11 plus", consisting of "intelligence tests" plus tests of mathematics and English, became feared as an ordeal by children and distrusted as unreliable and unfair by their parents.

Dissatisfaction with the workings of the secondary system, and admiration — perhaps misplaced — for the educational methods of America and Sweden, led to growing pressure for the adoption of a "comprehensive" system, in which the vast majority of children (with the exception of religious minorities) would go to the same "neighbourhood" schools. In this way, it was believed, children would be spared the arbitrary terrors of the "11 plus", and the barriers between social classes would gradually be broken down.

In 1964 the Labour government, which had taken up the cause of comprehensive education while in opposition, began to require local education authorities to submit plans for reorganizing their secondary schools on comprehensive lines. There were protests. In Liverpool a thousand grammar school pupils marched through the town centre. An angry local parent expressed a widely held view:

> The Labour Party is trying to make out that everyone is the same, but everyone is not the same. We want something more for our children than we had for ourselves. Our boy has done his bit by winning a place in a grammar school; we've organized our life to bring him up as a grammar school boy.

The words themselves show how passionately people felt. "Winning a place" suggests that those who went to secondary moderns were seen as "failures". "Organized our life"

shows the sort of sacrifices of time, money and convenience that parents were prepared to accept. "A grammar school boy" implies a quite distinctive type of person.

The Secretary of State for Education, Anthony Crosland, assured the public that

44 BC (before calculators) — maths lesson using mechanical calculating machines.

45 Boys operating an early computer — Sevenoaks School, 1964.

46 *The* **new university — Sussex, the library, 1964.**

47 Citizens of the Universe — learning about "Space" in a primary school.

the government "does not intend to force a rigid system of comprehensive schools on the country, but the Cabinet hopes a pattern will evolve."

A pattern did evolve, but it was a rather confused one. In some cases, it was confused by the issue of size. One of the subsidiary arguments for comprehensive schools was that, if they were large enough, then, even with an intake consisting largely of pupils of average and below-average ability, there would still be enough "bright" pupils to run a sixth form with a range of advanced courses to match those of any grammar school. But some critics feared that the massive schools created would become mere education factories, threatening and damaging to the average child, who needed to feel part of a community small enough for there to be a definite place for each individual.

Another problem was that, while some comprehensive schools were new, "purpose-built" institutions, with well-equipped buildings and specially-recruited staff, committed to the idea of change, others were simply grammar schools, re-named, which saw themselves as "going downhill", or secondary moderns, re-labelled, which saw the change as a cynical political fashion, or unhappy amalgamations of grammar and secondary moderns, sometimes on split-sites.

Nevertheless, the move went through. In 1960, comprehensive schools were very much the exception and by 1970, they were fast becoming the rule, though in the 1980s a few education authorities were still fighting a rearguard action to preserve what were, in effect and sometimes in name, their grammar schools.

Other Developments in Secondary Schools

There were other important developments in secondary education during the 1960s. Television became much more widely used as a teaching device and by 1969 the newly-established Inner London Education Authority's TV service was the largest closed-circuit network in the world. "Teaching machines" and computers also began to appear in schools and Britain's negotiations for entry to the Common Market increased interest in "language labs".

In 1964 it was decided that in 1970-71 the school-leaving age would be raised from 15 to 16. (In 1968 this was put off until 1973.) In 1965 the Certificate of Secondary Education (CSE) was introduced as a qualification for children "less able" than those normally taking the GCE O level. Meanwhile, the number of pupils actually taking O and A levels continued to rise steadily, as did the proportion staying on at school and going on to university or some other form of higher education (in each case by about 50%).

The Universities

If secondary schools grabbed the headlines in the early 1960s, the universities stole the limelight as the decade came to a close; but not, perhaps, in ways they would have wished. For higher education as a whole,

the period was one of rapid expansion, with the opening of a dozen new universities and the up-grading of eight Colleges of Advanced Technology (CATS) to university status. This expansion cost massive sums of public money and represented the official view that, in a competitive world, Britain's brains were its best resource and had to be developed to secure the nation's economic survival.

But not all the students saw things that way. Some objected strongly to the idea that their role was simply to serve as faceless "manpower" for "industry". Many, inspired by the philosophy of personal "liberation" and the revolution in life-styles which contemporary pop culture represented, saw themselves as leaders of a general movement against modern society and its supposed pressures towards conformism, consumerism and obedience to authority.

What became widely known in the press as "student protests" first broke out spectacularly at the London School of Economics in 1967, when students objected to the appointment of Walter Adams, former principal of the University College of Rhodesia, as director, alleging that he had not been sufficiently critical of the Ian Smith regime. The confrontation between the students and the authorities continued into 1968 and 1969, when militants forced the School to close for several days after breaking down newly-erected iron gates intended to prevent "sit-ins". By that time, "demos" and a "Revolutionary Festival" had also taken place at the new University of Essex, and student occupations had occurred at Hornsey and Guildford art colleges. Indeed, few major campuses had been entirely untouched by demands for greater student participation in the running of universities and colleges. But student politics soon showed itself to be very like most other kinds of politics — of interest only to a small minority of activists. Most students had other priorities. Consequently, the British scene paled in comparison with France,

where student riots merged into a general political upheaval which toppled General de Gaulle from power, or with Japan, where demonstrators burnt down the centre of the prestigious Tokyo University.

Primary Schools

Primary schools in Britain continued to attract the admiration of foreign visitors, both for their innovative architecture and for their "progressive" teaching methods, such as the Initial Teaching Alphabet, which introduced children to reading by banishing (temporarily at least) the oddities of English spelling so that children could concentrate on the relationship between script and sounds. In 1967 the report of a committee headed by Lady Plowden reminded the public that the brightest and the best in primary schooling was not necessarily

48 Small-group work in an open-plan classroom.

typical of the whole, and recommended the diversion of extra funds to certain Educational Priority Areas (EPAs) where school buildings were badly run down, books and equipment scanty, and nursery education needed drastic expansion if children were to get the best out of formal schooling.

The decade closed on a note of controversy, when the new Secretary of State for Education, Margaret Thatcher, announced the ending of free school milk for the under-7s and won herself the nickname "Ma Thatcher, Milk Snatcher". More people were to have reason to be grateful to Jennie Lee, Arts Minister in the outgoing Labour government, who saw her long-cherished dream of an "Open University" at last become a reality.

9 Sport

Soccer

In the 1960s soccer confirmed its position as *the* national sport, with a series of significant "firsts", records and "milestones". In 1961 Spurs became the first team to win the League and the Cup in the same season. (And they went on to win the Cup again in 1962 and 1967.) In the same year the player's maximum wage of £20 a week was abolished. A year later, Johnny Haynes, the Fulham and England captain, was earning £100 a week. 1962 saw not only the £100-a-week footballer, but also the first £100,000

transfer fee involving a British club, when Manchester United bought the Scottish striker Denis Law from the Italian club, Torino. Tony Hateley later became the first footballer to change from one British club (Aston Villa) to another (Chelsea) for the same sum.

49 Winners! Alf (later Sir Alf) Ramsey (left), the England manager, congratulates Manchester United's Nobby Styles (right) while captain Bobby Moore (West Ham) holds the coveted World Cup trophy.

	FA Cup	League Championship	League Cup
1960-1	Spurs	Spurs	Aston Villa
1961-2	Spurs	Ipswich	Norwich City
1962-3	Man. Utd.	Everton	Birmingham City
1963-4	West Ham	Liverpool	Leicester City
1964-5	Liverpool	Man. Utd.	Chelsea
1965-6	Everton	Liverpool	W.B.Albion
1966-7	Spurs	Man. Utd.	Q.P.R.
1967-8	W.B.Albion	Man. City	Leeds
1968-9	Man. City	Leeds	Swindon
1969-70	Chelsea	Everton	Man. City

In 1963 Spurs also became the first British club to win the European Cup Winners Cup. West Ham repeated their triumph in 1965 and Manchester City did the same in 1970. In 1967 Glasgow Celtic, who dominated Scottish football throughout the 1960s, became the first British club to win the European Cup; the following year Manchester United became the first English club to do so. But, if British clubs at last began to show signs of taking European competitions seriously and of adopting a "continental" style of play which was both more "fluid" and less "physical", they still seemed unable to compete, club for club, with such giants as Real Madrid, Barcelona, Benfica, A. C. Milan and Inter-Milan.

Nationally, it was another matter. In 1966, for the first time, and before a television audience estimated at 400,000,000, England won the World Cup, thanks largely to Geoff Hurst, who became the first player ever to score a hat-trick in a World Cup final.

At club level, other records were also established. In 1964 Jimmy Dickinson of Portsmouth became the first player to make more than 700 League appearances for his club, and in the following year the veteran winger Stanley Matthews became the first footballer to be knighted for his services to the sport. Alf Ramsey, the England team manager, was to be knighted in 1967 and Matt Busby, the Manchester United manager, in 1968. Jimmy Greaves proved himself goal-scorer of the decade, with a record tally of 357 First Division goals, including no fewer than six hat-tricks for Chelsea in the 1960-61 season and four for Spurs in each of the seasons 1962-63, 1963-64 and 1968-69. In 1970, Bobby Charlton made his 106th appearance for England, to set a new record as most-capped player.

But success was not the same as progress. The spread of car and TV ownership gave more and more fans the chance of seeing, directly or on the screen, the top teams and players in action. And while this confirmed the popularity of successful major sides like Leeds and Liverpool, who could now number among their "local" fans people who lived fifty or more miles away, it also began to undermine support for Third and Fourth Division sides, who lacked "glamour", not to mention modern grounds and facilities. The transfer of Martin Peters from West Ham to Spurs for £200,000 in 1970 seemed to confirm the power of money over the game. And the problem of "violence on the terraces" emerged as a persistent curse, which threatened to damage the reputation of individual clubs and the standing of soccer itself.

Rugby and Cricket

Rugby in the 1960s remained the supreme province of the Welsh, whose splendid national side included such legendary figures as Barry John and Gareth Edwards. Cricket, by contrast, produced little to thrill the spectator. Yorkshire won the county championship with monotonous regularity (1960, 1962, 1963, 1966, 1967, 1968), but the introduction of commercially-sponsored, one-day "cup" competitions from 1963 onwards did add a new note of interest. And so did politics.

When Basil d'Oliveira, a South African Cape Coloured, and probably the most proficient all-rounder of his day, was picked as a member of the England team to tour South Africa in the winter of 1968-69, the South African premier objected to his selection, on the grounds that it was "political" — in other words, a deliberately provocative challenge to South Africa's apartheid policy of racially-segregated sport. The English cricketing authorities took the view that d'Oliveira had been selected purely on merit, and that it was not up to any outside body to tell them whom they could or could not choose to represent England. They therefore refused to back down on the issue and the tour was cancelled. Proposals for a South African tour of England then became the subject of further controversy, as a "Stop the Seventy Tour" campaign disrupted cricket matches with noisy demonstrations which enraged lovers of the game but succeeded in their main objective. There was no Seventy Tour, and South Africa entered a long period of isolation from international cricket.

Britain at the Olympics

At Olympic level, Britain's athletes could offer little apart from inspired individual performances. Rome in 1960 saw gold medals for Don Thompson in the 50-kilometre walk and for Anita Lonsbrough in the 200-metre breast-stroke. It also saw the arrival on the

50 "Stop the Seventy Tour" — and a decade later sporting links with South Africa remained a subject of fierce controversy.

international scene of a young heavy-weight boxer called Cassius Clay, soon to be known as Muhammad Ali. At Tokyo in 1964 the British tally of golds rose to four, with Welshman Lynn Davies gaining Britain's first gold for a field event since 1908 and Mary Rand winning Britain's first ever women's athletic gold — both for the long jump. The high-altitude Olympics of 1968, denounced by one athlete as "a triangular match between Kenya, Ethiopia and Mexico", nevertheless saw five golds for Britain — in boxing, yachting, clay-pigeon shooting, three-day eventing and the 400-metres hurdles, for which David Hemery set a new world record.

Sporting Moments of the 1960s

In other sports, too, there were individual heroes and moments of passing glory. In 1963, Henry Cooper knocked down Muhammad Ali in the fourth round of their heavy-weight contest, but was too badly cut about the eyes to press home his advantage. He also lost their return bout in 1966. In tennis, only Ann Haydon-Jones could offer a challenge to the dominance of the Australians, winning the Ladies Singles titles at Wimbledon in 1970. In motor racing, Britain fared better, with Jim Clark becoming world champion in 1965. Golf saw the rise of Tony Jacklin as a British superstar. In 1969 he won the British Open, the first British player to do so for eighteen years, and in 1970 he went on to win the US Open as well.

Participation Sports

At the level of actual participation, soccer, cricket and tennis retained their well-established popularity, while new sports, such as squash, canoeing and karate, gained in numbers and appeal. By 1968, for instance, there were more than 250 karate clubs in Britain and the country could boast a team of world-class standards. But neither darts nor snooker had yet become the focus for big-money tournaments and TV spectaculars. And although many people went running for fitness and pleasure, the American cult of jogging had yet to be born.

The establishment of a Ministry of Sport and a Sports Council signified growing official recognition that sport could contribute to the health and well-being of the nation. But the early researches of the Sports Council soon showed just how inadequate the provision of public facilities still was. As the 1960s came to a close, it was estimated that Britain still needed almost 500 swimming pools, more than 800 sports centres and around 1,000 golf courses.

51 Tony Jacklin — Britain's first golf-superstar for a generation.

10 Newcomers

During the 1960s immigration stopped being just a fact of life in Britain and started to become a political issue. There was nothing new about immigration as such. After all, the British themselves were the descendants of Celtic tribesmen, Roman legionaries, Saxon farmers, Danish raiders, Norman knights, Flemish weavers and Huguenot craftsmen -- to name but a few. Since the mid-nineteenth century, Britain had received hundreds of thousands of Irish fleeing poverty and tens of thousands of Jews fleeing persecution. In the inter-war period it had accepted refugees from fascism and, in the years after the war, its victims.

It would be easy to say that what was different about post-war immigration was that the immigrants were not white. But it would not be true. Many Roman legionaries were undoubtedly not white, and London's black population goes back at least to the sixteenth century. There have been Muslim and Chinese communities in Britain since the early nineteenth century. What was perhaps different about the post-war period was that immigrants who were not white or nominally Christian began, for the first time, to outnumber those who were.

Some were ex-servicemen who had come to Britain during the course of the Second World War and decided to stay on afterwards. Some were refugees, driven from their homelands by the bloodshed and terror which accompanied the division of India and Pakistan. But most, wherever they came from, were, like the 498 West Indians who arrived on the *Empire Windrush* in 1948, looking for work. The great majority were men, without wives, children or relatives. And Britain, short of manpower and anxious to re-build its war-shattered economy, was glad to have them.

During the 1950s the numbers of immigrants from South Asia, the West Indies and Africa gradually increased. Quite a number of them were white families of British origin, returning from employment in colonies which were now independent countries. Over the course of the decade, about a quarter of a million Irish also moved in to Britain, continuing a tradition more than 200 years old. And the Hungarian rising of 1956 added another 20,000 refugees. So the non-whites were a minority of the new arrivals until the 1960s.

In 1958 there were street-fights between black and white people in Nottingham and in Notting Hill Gate, London. The courts handed out stiff sentences to offenders found guilty of violence. But a note of alarm had been sounded. Immigration, or rather its effects, had suddenly become a "problem". There were calls for controls to be imposed on the flow of immigrants and Acts of Parliament were duly passed in 1962 and 1968. In each case, the effect of the Acts in the short run was to increase the flow of immigrants, as would-be arrivals rushed to beat the deadline. In 1965 and 1968 Acts of Parliament were also passed to try to ensure that British citizens, whatever their colour, were not denied fair treatment in such matters as housing and employment.

In 1958 the Home Office had estimated

52 Wojjer mean, immigrants? We was all born 'ere!

53 Learning together.

that the number of coloured people in Britain from the Commonwealth was around 210,000, of whom more than half were West Indians, a quarter from India and Pakistan and a tenth from West Africa. According to the 1966 Sample Census, the total immigrant population of Britain was around 2,500,000, or about 5% of the total population, but of these just under a third were from Eire and just over a third from outside the Commonwealth (chiefly Poland, Italy, Russia, Germany). In other words, less than one million, or less than 2% were coloured.

Nevertheless, fears that immigration threatened the British way of life did not diminish. One reason for this may have been the terrible race-riots which devastated American cities in the mid-1960s. Scenes of looting, shooting and burning appeared nightly on British television screens, and many people perhaps asked themselves: "Could it happen here?" In 1968 the then Conservative politician Enoch Powell predicted that it could. Edward Heath, the Conservative leader, made it very clear that Mr Powell's remarks were unwelcome and that, if and when the Conservatives came to power again, Mr Powell could not expect to get a government post. But 100,000 people wrote to Mr Powell about his speech, and the overwhelming majority did so to congratulate him on speaking out. Very few of the letters were abusive towards racial minorities; by far the greater number simply expressed fear or confusion; where fears involving jobs or housing were expressed, they were usually at odds with the facts. Some thought that the newcomers would be a burden on the economy and social services. But, in fact, the population of economically active persons was far higher among the immigrant population than among the host society, for very few were children and even fewer were old people. (In 1966 only 11% of the immigrant population was over 45.) Some of Mr Powell's correspondents were concerned that Britain was simply becoming overcrowded. But, in fact, the net balance of migration had shifted significantly in the course of the 1960s. Whereas, between 1961 and 1963, 316,000 more people had entered Britain than had left it, between 1964 and 1968 the country registered a net loss of more than 361,000 persons.

Perhaps the false impression of massive numbers of "New Commonwealth" migrants was derived from the fact that a high proportion of the newcomers lived close together, in the poorer "inner-city" zones of London, Birmingham, Wolverhampton, Bradford, and Huddersfield, though, in fact, many smaller towns, such as Bedford and High Wycombe, were just as cosmopolitan. Most of these New Commonwealth newcomers did manual work, like the Irish, in factories or on building sites. But they also supplied a high proportion of transport workers. Large numbers worked in the health service, not only as cleaners and orderlies, but also as nurses and doctors. Many of the Asians set up their own businesses, especially in the clothing industries and shopkeeping. But professional and managerial positions proved harder to come by.

Problems Faced by the Immigrant Communities

Whatever their economic success — and for most it was hard won and a great source of satisfaction — most of the newcomers felt themselves strangers in a strange land. This experience may have been most puzzling for the West Indians who spoke English, came from a Christian-based culture and were used to British laws and institutions. Muslims, Sikhs and Hindus, by contrast, showed a strong desire to keep alive their customs and culture and sense of distinctive identity.

But many of the newcomers were not newcomers at all. As early as 1966, most of the children living in Britain whose parents were from India, Sri Lanka, the West Indies or West Africa, had themselves been born in Britain. Problems of identity and adjustment were perhaps faced most acutely by those

54 No need to bring the fans — they're already here. West Indies cricket supporters, 1966.

55 Staff at Greenwich District Hospital, 1969 —
on both sides of the counter.

who had come to Britain as children or
teenagers, or who had known no other home.

Immigrant parents were usually very
eager for their children to take advantage of
the educational opportunities available in
Britain. But British schools were not always
what they expected them to be. Many
thought that the teachers were too easy-
going, giving the younger children too much
play and the older ones too little discipline.
School meals sometimes caused problems for
Hindus, who would not eat beef, and
Muslims, who would not eat pork, bacon or
ham. Uniforms and the kit worn for P.E. and
games likewise caused problems for many
Asian families, whose standards of decency
required girls to keep their legs and arms

covered at all times. School activities and
lessons, too, could be a source of unexpected
difficulties, even at the primary level. Not
every parent felt able to let his or her child
take part in a Nativity play. And many
children came from families who did not
regard dancing as a respectable pastime.

56 Promised Land? — Asians fleeing Kenya arrive
at Heathrow, 1968.

66

Teachers often lacked the knowledge and experience to cope with these situations. And it was the children who got caught in the cross-fire.

Most managed to survive very well, often mastering the language faster than their parents and thus being able to help them deal with doctors, officials, form-filling, shopping and other everyday tasks. Perhaps because they had been to school in Britain and had British friends, they often found it easier to see things from the British point of view. Sometimes, this caused conflict within families. Many Asian and West Indian parents felt that British youngsters had far too casual an attitude towards authority in general, and towards the authority of parents in particular. Others disapproved of easy mixing between teenage boys and girls, the acceptance of discos and pubs as normal places of entertainment, and the apparent general indifference to religion.

Numerous surveys were carried out to find out what the young people (aged 13-19) themselves thought about it all:

"We came in winter . . . . As soon as I returned home from school it got dark. I got stuck in the house all the time. In Jullundur I was used to playing out in the streets until ten, eleven at night. It was a big change for me, here. Life was all boring. I had no friends. My sisters and I sat inside and watched television." (Hindu boy)

"I don't mind assemblies or the bible class. But I call myself a Hindu. I keep reminding myself of the tales of Rama and Krishna that my mother has told me . . . . English boys are not interested . . . all they're interested in is sports". (Hindu boy)

"My mother reads Sikh scriptures everyday. But my parents don't force me to do so. I'm beginning to forget the Sikh

57 Promised Land? — Liverpool.

prayers I used to know in India . . . . I go to the gurdwara once in a fortnight, maybe.'' (Sikh boy)

"Sitting on the floor in a gurdwara, I get cramped . . . . And the service goes on all morning: five hours: They should modernise Sikhism. Look at the Christian churches . . . they're trying to attract the young — all those Salvation Army pop groups . . . . I've been to Christian churches both Protestant and Catholic. I like their services. At least I understand what they're saying.'' (Sikh boy)

"I read the Holy Koran as often as I can. There's a copy at home in Arabic, with pronunciations in Urdu written under each line . . . . I tell this to my religious teacher and English boys, but they don't bother. People don't care for religion in this country.'' (Muslim boy)

"Yes, I've eaten pork and bacon. I don't like it. Its too greasy. Of course, my parents don't know. They'd be appalled if they knew. They don't even buy margarine because someone told them it had pig's fat in it.'' (Muslim boy)

"The history books here say all the good things the English did in India, not a word about all the bad things they did.'' (Sikh boy)

"When I have a quarrel or something with a class mate, the first thing that comes out of her mouth is "You black bitch!'' I mean girls whom you treat as friends. This colour thing is very deep.'' (Hindu girl)

"West Indians are refusing to be brought up-to-date in England by their own child-ren. They remain more Victorian than the oldest, most reactionary British them-selves.'' (Jamaican boy)

". . . following this pop thing. That's stupid. It's a waste of money . . . . They sort of pick up the habits from these pop stars, about drugs and smoking, the whole lot, and they just can't afford it really.'' (Hindu boy)

"I applied for a lot of jobs . . . but every interview I went to they would sit there and look at you . . . . They'd give you a cup of tea and after ten minutes they'd say goodbye, and you knew when you left you wouldn't get the job.'' (Hindu boy)

". . . just something inside me that wants to go back. I still want to stay here, all the opportunities going round here. But it's just something inside me that's saying 'You've got to go back.' '' (Hindu boy)

Despite the tensions, most of the newcomers managed to work out a way of life for them-selves. In Asian families, respect for parents remained strong, and most young people continued to be willing to enter arranged marriages. At the same time, the ethnic minority communities themselves became more balanced in terms of age and sex, because the immigration regulations, which limited the numbers of adult male workers, allowed in the wives, children and aged relatives of those who had already made their homes in Britain. Links with the home-land could also be kept up by post and cheap charter-flights. But, while the idea of "going back" seemed possible to many parents, for more and more of the children, home was Stockport or Peterborough, rather than Sylhet or the Punjab.

Date List

1960	Harold Macmillan's "Wind of Change" speech
	Birth of Prince Andrew
	Marriage of Princess Margaret
	Rome Olympics
1961	Rudolf Nureyev defects from USSR
	World's first hovercraft service begins
1962	Cuban missile crisis
	First Beatles hit record
1963	Britain pioneers electricity from nuclear power
	"Great Train Robbery"
	Assassination of John F. Kennedy
1964	Birth of Prince Edward
	Tokyo Olympics
	Labour wins general election
1965	Death of Sir Winston Churchill
	Anti-Communist massacres in Indonesia
	"UDI" in Northern Rhodesia (Zimbabwe)
1966	Labour win general election
	England win soccer World Cup
	Kwame Nkrumah falls from power in Ghana
1967	Sir Francis Chichester completes single-handed voyage round the world
	"Six-Day War" in the Middle East
	Military sieze power in Greece
	Devaluation of £
	Colour TV introduced in Britain
1968	Civil rights marches in Northern Ireland
	Russian intervention in Czechoslovakia
	Mass student demonstrations in USA, France, Japan
	Mexico Olympics
1969	Investiture of the Prince of Wales
	First moon landing
1970	Conservatives win general election

Books for Further Reading

Ronald Blythe, *Akenfield: Portrait of an English Village*, Allen Lane/Penguin, 1969
Peter Calvocoressi, *The British Experience 1945-75*, Penguin, 1979
Ken Coates and Richard Silburn, *Poverty: The Forgotten Englishmen*, Penguin, 1973
D. Elliston Allen, *British Tastes*, 1969
Ronald Fletcher, *The Family and Marriage in Britain*, Penguin, 1966
Ronald Frankenburg, *Communities in Britain*, Penguin, 1966
J. H. Goldthorpe, *The Affluent Worker*, Cambridge University Press, 1968
Josephine Klein, *Samples from English Cultures*, Routledge, 1965
Ernest Krauss, *Ethnic Minorities in Britain*, 1971
Bernard Levin, *The Pendulum Years: Britain and the Sixties*, Cape/Pan, 1970
George Melly, *Revolt into Style: the pop arts in Britain*, 1970
Trevor Noble, *Modern Britain: Structure & Change*, Batsford, 1975
Raymond Williams, *Communications*, Chatto/Penguin, 1966
Barbara Wootton, *Contemporary Britain: 3 Lectures*, 1971

Index

The numbers in **bold type** refer to the figure numbers of the illustrations

Aberfan 16; **12**
affluence 6, 20-1; **15**
Africa 5, 10-12, 23, 24, 61, 64; **9**

Beatles 32-4; **27, 28, 29**
Berlin Wall 13
birth control 7, 25 ·
Bloom, John 10
Bond, James 7, 52
BBC 7, 27, 48-51

Chichester, Sir Francis 10; **8**
China 12, 13
Churchill, Sir Winston 19; **14**
cinema 52
computers 7; **45**
Concorde 14
crime 16, 19, 20-1, 40-2, 48
Cuba 6, 13
Czechoslovakia 13

decimalization 7; **4**
de Gaulle, General Charles 19, 58
divorce 21, 25-6
Dylan, Bob 6, 44

ecology 6, 14
economic problems 21-3, 24; **18**
education 20, 54-8, 66; **4, 43, 44, 45, 46, 47, 48, 52, 53**
Eichmann, Adolf 10
EEC 9, 22, 23

fashion 35-8; **21, 29, 30, 31**
food 30-1; **25, 30, 31**
France 9, 13, 21, 38, 57

Gaitskell, Hugh 23
gambling 39-40
Germany, West 13, 21
Greece 13

Heath, Edward 24, 64
hippies 6, 43
housing 27-30; **22, 23, 24**
hovercraft 13

Kennedy, Mrs Jacqueline 10
Kennedy, Robert F. 13, 19; **13**

Liverpool 47, 55, 60; **57**
London 8, 10, 16, 19, 24, 27, 37-8, 47, 48, 63

Macmillan, Harold 5, 20, 23
Middle East 12
Mods and Rockers 6, 47; **2, 3, 32, 34**
moon landing 7, 13-14; **10**

nuclear disarmament 23, 24; **20**
nuclear power 13
Nureyev, Rudolf 10

permissiveness 6, 25, 39-47; **36**
pollution 15, 16
poverty 23; **16**
protests 5, 8-9, 24-5, 57; **5, 6, 20, 38, 50**

Quant, Mary 37; **30**
Queen Elizabeth 19, 47, 48; **7**
QE11 14; **11**

regionalism 27
Rhodesia 24, 57
Royal Family 10; **7, 37**

Scotland 24, 29, 47
soccer 59-60; **49**
"Space Race" 13; **10**
sport 51-2, 59-62, 67; **49, 50, 51, 54**
"Swinging Sixties" 5; **29, 36**

technology 7; **19, 45**
television 48-52, 57, 60, 64, 67; **26, 39, 40, 41**
thalidomide 15
theatre 42-3
Third World 6, 10; **9**

Ulster 24-5
unemployment 21, 23
USSR 10, 13, 16, 19
UN 15
USA 12, 13, 24, 31, 34, 37, 51, 62, 64

Vietnam 8, 12, 24; **6**
violence 6
VSO 6

Wales 10, 16, 24, 29, 61
Wilson, Harold 22, 23, 24, 47
women 25-6, 31, 40
Woolwich, Bishop of 6

youth 6-7, 20-1, 32, 47, 51, 67-8; **1, 2, 3, 6, 19, 21, 26, 32, 34, 37**